Getting Divorced from Mother & Dad

Getting Divorced

from Mother & Dad

THE DISCOVERIES OF
THE FISCHER-HOFFMAN PROCESS

Bob Hoffman

E. P. Dutton & Co., Inc.
New York

First Edition

10 9 8 7 6 5 4 3 2 1

Library of Congress Cataloging in Publication Data

Hoffman, Robert, 1932-
Getting divorced from mother & dad.
1. Fantasy—Therapeutic use. 2. Love. 3. Self-respect.
4. Self-actualization. I. Title.
RC489.F35H63 1976 158'.1 76–15378

ISBN: 0–525–11328–2

Published simultaneously in Canada by Clarke, Irwin & Company Limited, Toronto and Vancouver
Designed by The Etheredges

I lovingly dedicate
this book to the living spirit of
Dr. Siegfried Fischer,
scientist, neurologist and psychiatrist
of great wisdom and
deep compassion for mankind.

Contents

Foreword

Some years ago Donovan Bess, then a *San Francisco Chronicle* reporter, introduced me to Bob Hoffman. At that time Bob was offering his services in an eight-session process in which he employed himself as a psychic, assisting his clients toward an expansion of love.

When I came upon him I had been through many therapies and "worked things out," so I did not expect a dramatic experience. Yet at the end I had to agree with Bob that never before had I formed such a coherent picture of the action of parental influences in my development. As I look back after four years, I continue to regard it as a significant impact in my life.

It seemed to me, going through this process, that even though Bob was a gifted healer of souls, the success of his work did not rest upon this personal ingredient alone. His therapeutic guided trip—a well-organized package of procedures comprising the analysis of early experiences, abreaction, and extensive use of imagery—seemed to me a technical conception that could be further developed and effectively used by others, without his psychic ability.

Within a short time I was employing a group adaptation of the process (which I called the "Fischer-Hoffman Process," a name that it has retained) in a group for psychological and spiritual development that I led at the time—the beginnings of

Seekers After Truth (SAT). The results seemed good enough to invite further exploration, and months later my collaborators, Rosalyn Shaffer and Kathleen Speeth, were employing the method in two other SAT groups. Bob attended Rosalyn's group as an observer, and though he disapproved in many regards, he appreciated the workability of the group application. Bob then generated an alternative form. His way was better in his hands than our attempt had been, and proof of my conviction is that some two hundred people in SAT groups have experienced Bob's approach as part of their program, either under his direction or that of his apprentices.

The Fischer-Hoffman wave has now gone from coast to coast and even as far as Chile and Spain, Israel and India, and I am happy to believe that I have incurred some good karma by playing John the Baptist in this story.

Months ago, I was invited by Michael Toms, director of New Dimensions, to participate in a public meeting and broadcast in San Francisco with Bob and several psychologists. Addressing myself in answer to a question as to what I regarded as characteristic of the Fischer-Hoffman process, I made the following statement:

> There has been a tendency in psychotherapy ever since the dawn of psychoanalysis to emphasize the therapeutic aspects of unstructured situations. To begin with, psychoanalysis was built around the technique of free association, a situation in which a person says whatever comes to mind. Whatever the value of interpretation, there is value in free association (which is a relinquishing of structure) because in the ordinary social situation, we are, in one way or another, playing a game with implicit rules.
>
> The therapeutic aspects of unstructuring have culminated in encounter groups and similar situations where a group of people meet without rules in an open situation that summons the creative aspects of the person.
>
> As distinct from this most predominant therapeutic tendency, the Fischer-Hoffman Process is highly structured. I believe that this is a time in which there are so many strategies which are known in psychotherapy that it is possible to package a process where these are systematically included.

Another aspect of the Process, as I see it, is its being in many ways counter counter-culture. The counter-culture has emphasized the here-and-now and disdained the past, for instance, and the Fischer-Hoffman approach takes us back to the past, just as psychoanalysis did at the beginning. Freud's original insight was that people who suffered from neurosis are suffering from memories. So the intent of therapy was to elucidate these memories and their associations. The chief concept of psychoanalysis is, perhaps, that of transference. Our relationships with people are not only seen as transference in the sense that they are the re-enactment of the parental relationships, but in that they fall short of the fullness of life. We are not living if we are acting as automatons according to programming. So the early psychoanalytic attempt was to understand transference by analyzing the parental situation.

Yet in recent years, psychotherapy has moved more and more into understanding and repairing the present. Gestalt therapy, which is the approach that I have practiced most, was, I think, the most significant voice in bringing about a cultural understanding of this. The here-and-now came to stand in opposition to the endless elucidation of the past. And yet, Fritz Perls, the creator of Gestalt therapy, had many, if not most, of his greatest successes, I believe, when he would follow the thread from present to past and work on what was happening with one or the other of the parents. So that even though Gestalt embraced the here and—now ideologically, in practice—it absorbed much of psychoanalysis. If the creed of Gestalt Therapy were to be taken literally, this approach would miss the working out of the past. I believe, like Bob, that our capacity to love others is rooted in our ability to love ourselves, and that this goes hand in hand with the state of our relationships with our parents.

I know Bob to be a good storyteller, and hope that his gift as a communicator brings some of his healing influence to you.

CLAUDIO NARANJO

Acknowledgments

I want to express my love and heartfelt gratitude to the two people who worked so closely with me in bringing this work to its present form. This book would not be what it is without the skillful and imaginative writing assistance of Dennis Briskin, and the perceptiveness, editorial ability and profound understanding of the Fischer-Hoffman Process of my dedicated associate, Marion Pastor.

My thanks also go to Dr. Claudio Naranjo, Kathleen Speeth and Rosalyn Shaffer for their support of my work, and for opening the doors to the group concept; to Dr. Ernest Pecci for his early recognition of the value of the Fischer-Hoffman Process; to Michael Hoffman, my beloved son, Harold Oemke, Rose Paul, and Debra Smith for their loving encouragement to create the book; and to Reverend Rose Strongin, a loving spiritual minister who with patience and understanding opened me to my natural sensory perception.

Further thanks to my friends Irwin and Eileen Salk and Dr. Stephen Karpman for their enthusiastic encouragement.

My grateful appreciation, also, to my early "psychic therapy" clients, whose participation helped develop the Fischer-Hoffman Process.

Finally, my sincere thanks to Bill Whitehead of E. P. Dutton for his patient, skillful assistance at every stage of this project.

God Bless With Love.
Bob Hoffman

Getting Divorced from Mother & Dad

1. How's Your Love Life?

Asking about your love life is a rude way to begin a book. On the other hand, it does cut through the bullshit to get to what matters: how you are living your life right now.

This book is filled with rude, provocative questions to help you see yourself as you are. While looking honestly may be difficult and sometimes painful, the reward is worth it because seeing it all is the only way to start resolving it.

Fear of the pain blinds us to the goal of healing. Only by seeing your problems clearly and experiencing them can you do something about them. There really is a way to arrive at something better than life as you may have known it, no matter how stuck you may feel, no matter how completely you may have given in to despair—even if only periodically. There is a way out. Others before you have done it and gone on to lives of peace, with no inner conflicts or anxieties. So can you.

The way out begins by answering the question: How *is* your love life? Do you have warm, loving people in your life? People who know you well and love you? People you know well and love in return? Is that circle of love expanding as you meet new people? Do you give and receive love easily with persons of either sex? Is there someone special with whom you share the kind of sex life you deeply want?

Above all, do you love yourself? Do you like yourself totally and feel comfortable with who you are and what you do? Or are you in conflict with yourself, liking yourself some of the time while not liking yourself the rest of the time? Are you able to nurture yourself with compassion and understanding when you fall short of being perfect? Do you give to yourself as well as to others?

If things are not the way you want them to be, do you know why? If you are not drawing to yourself the kind of people you want, do you know what's wrong? How many people who were important in your life five years ago are still around? How many of those who are important to you now will still be with you a year from now? Do you really enjoy whom you are with and what you do? Is your life the way you want it to be?

If it is not, do you understand why your life works this way? (If you don't know, this book may help you find out, while pointing you toward doing something about it.)

Think a moment about your answers to the questions above. . . . If you are unreservedly happy with what came to mind as you read the questions, and your love life is beautiful, that's great! For you life is probably a great and glorious adventure of spiritual, emotional, intellectual, and physical fulfillment. Which puts you among the "abnormal" 2 per cent who know how to give and receive love.

The other 98 per cent are not so fortunate. For them something is wrong; terribly wrong. The love they dream of never quite becomes reality. They meet, barely touch and move on, like stones skipping across still water. Or they have love affairs that begin well enough, perhaps even quite intensely, but eventually fizzle out, if not sooner then later. Their marriages aren't doing well, either. What was once the culmination of their hopes for love is becoming more and more a battle ground. Even the best marriages between "healthy" persons are falling apart, either through divorce or by continuing in name only. Husbands, wives, friends, lovers, brothers, sisters, parents, and children are groping and wondering to themselves, "Whatever happened to love? Is it just a childhood fantasy?"

Certainly not. That love life you have wished for, or struggled in vain to create, is not just a dream of idealistic youth. Nor is love just a word. It really is possible to love and be loved beautifully, not just for a moment but for the rest of your life.

Love is not only possible, it is natural. We were created for love and to love. Nothing is more real than love; and nothing is more painful than its absence.

Compounding the problem is that love seems to be all around us. We see, hear, and read about love (or its substitutes) almost everywhere. Much of this subtle and overt stimulation helps foster in us an intense desire to experience love. We want love, and we want to be loved—there's no use denying it, even to ourselves.

All of which serves to heighten our disappointment and frustration at not achieving love. With all that is being written and said about love and human relationships, many people are well informed on the need for love and the consequences of not attaining it. They know they need to be more genuinely loving of themselves and others. They hear it in sermons, see it in the movies, read it in books and magazines, and hear it on the radio. The idea has been all around us for a long time. Anyone who isn't living in a cave or on a deserted island can tell you that—as the song says—what the world needs now is love.

If love is difficult to find, it is not for lack of searching. Many people work hard to get love. One common way is to become attractive, spend time in places in which other searchers are found, and wait for the right person to come along. Often people do this while kidding themselves that love depends on finding the right person with an attractive mix of good qualities and a minimum of bad ones.

"If only I could find a good-looker with brains and a sense of humor," he kids himself, "it would be easy enough to love."

"If only I could find a tender man who knows how to make a living and wants to have a family," she kids herself, "love would be no problem."

The popular image of the ideal man and woman changes with the times, so what they look for changes. Nonetheless, the delusion behind this kind of attitude is that until they meet someone who fulfills their expectations they have to withhold love from the world.

The variety and mobility of people in our large urban areas only perpetuates the false hopes of those who look for someone "out there" to release the love inside them. While it is true that each new day is a fresh chance to find that "wonderful" person who will make the dream happen, it is also true that for those who cannot love, each new day is likely to be a replay of a familiar disappointment and emptiness. Life often becomes a struggle when we start with a false assumption and then try to make it true. Many lonely, unloved people assume that finding the right person is what they need in order to love.

Love is up to you, not *them.* If your love life is terrible, it isn't because . . . (Fill in the blank with whatever excuses you've been giving yourself: "It's hard to meet people." "I'm not good-looking enough." "I don't have enough money." "I don't like hanging around bars making phony talk." "There's nobody my type around here." "Nobody wants a divorced woman with kids," and so forth.)

While many people are mistakenly looking for another person to open them to love, others are seeking love through prayer and religion. They believe that if they pray a lot and act "good" that somehow God, maybe through a miracle or through one of the lesser angels, will open their hearts to love. In the Western world there has been a long line of ministers, rabbis, teachers, and lay preachers encouraging and admonishing us with the power and beauty of love.

"God is love," they tell us. "Love thy neighbor as thyself." "Love conquers all." "God so loved the world He gave His only begotten son," and so forth.

While love is powerful and beautiful, and the religious experience can be glorious, it hardly does much good for those who don't know how to love. Much of what we know as religion is preaching and admonitions, which only cause more confusion, discomfort, and guilt. After all, says the "sinner," if I won't listen to the voice of God, then I must really be hopelessly lost —and *really* unworthy of love. The result is more guilt, not more love.

The problem with religion as a path to love is that it commands people to act in a way that is only meaningful when done out of free choice. Love cannot be ordered. While it is possible to order people to behave *as if* they loved their neighbors, no amount of admonitions or threats will cause them to feel a love they do not feel. The secret guilt of many apparently pious persons stems from this truth. Inside themselves they know they don't feel the love they were told to feel. Tragically, they often feel guilty and try harder. They look at the examples of Moses, Jesus, Mohammed, Buddha, or some other saintly person and attempt to be like their spiritual hero. But they can't *be* their love heroes; they can only be *like* them, which means they are imitating someone else instead of being themselves.

It is not only Christianity and Judaism that have this problem. Many have turned away from Western religion to Eastern religions, particularly Buddhism and its variants. In this time of instability, confusion, and uncertainty gurus and other spiritual masters have considerable influence. It is possible to sit before a guru and have the experience of receiving his warmth, blessing, and knowledge. You can sit there all day long, join his ashram, follow him from here to India and back while getting a daily injection of his spiritual love. This doesn't make you a lover, although the appearance can be convincing.

No spiritual journey, however high or enlightened, is sufficient to teach love. Like a kite in the air, the spirit may soar with the guidance of the master, but the rest of the self remains on the ground, holding the string and watching.

This is not to say that the valuable teachings of the East should be ignored. Those who wish to understand the thought and experience of the mystics should search for the truths they contain. But they should be aware that it is an illusion to think that one can learn self-love by sitting before a mystic. And remember that it isn't nearly as difficult to love God, who is perfect, as it is to love the real men and women who sit next to you while you pray or meditate.

A word here about meditation. As a technique of relaxation and tension relief it is marvelous, and some people have great insights or spiritual experiences while meditating. While many people certainly need to relax and calm themselves as a means to better health and a more positive life, those who meditate as a means to love are in danger of confusing cause and effect. People do not fail to give and receive love because they are tired and tense. The truth is just the opposite. It is their inability to love themselves and others that leads to tension, fatigue, irritability, and all the other physical and emotional symptoms meditation helps relieve.

The love of self and others takes place on the emotional level of our beings, while the love of God through prayer is spiritual. In the same way that people with emotional limitations sometimes overdevelop their intellects to compensate for their deficiencies, highly religious people are often struggling to make up for their emotional problems by overdeveloping their spirituality. Each of us is a Trinity of intellect, emotions, and spirit within a physical body. Thus, while there is nothing wrong with developing your spirituality, it is a mistake to think that more and more spirituality will enable you to love yourself and others on the emotional level. A commune full of highly spiritual vegetarians who have never learned to love themselves is no more loving than an apartment complex of swinging singles who poison and anesthetize themselves with alcohol and tobacco to avoid their inner pain. The appearance is highly different, while the inner reality is often the same: no love.

This is not to put down communes or other experiments with unconventional living arrangements. A few communes have been successful because of the true loving nature of the persons involved. The 2 per cent who love themselves selflessly and can send that love to others easily and naturally from the core of their being can accomplish almost anything they set their mind, body, spirit, and emotions to doing. Their success comes from who they are, however, not the form they have chosen to live by.

While much of this sounds highly negative, it is by no means despairing or pessimistic. Beneath the surface of your negativity there is a perfect diamond. By removing the encrusted dirt from your diamond, your real, loving self can be set free.

In order to get there, however, it is first necessary to show where the false paths lead us. The proof is not in my argument but in your own experience. Ask yourself if finding the right person, experiencing religiosity, or meditating have taught you to love yourself and others. If you are honest with yourself, you will see that none of these activities, however beneficial and well-intentioned, gets to the emotional problem of love.

Since lovelessness is an emotional problem, many people have gone searching through the maze of psychotherapies for the solution. Psychotherapy is gaining greater acceptance all the time, along with the various tangents of the human potential movement. Many forms of therapy, using a myriad of techniques, have been devised, ranging from encounter groups to one-to-one therapy to quasi-spiritual religious disciplines. You can talk or listen, scream or be screamed at, told to think or not to think, be stroked, doped, joked, or poked. Some of these therapies even directly approach the problem of loving self and others—but when they do, it's usually with admonitions and encouragement, which are not of lasting value.

As with other approaches, psychotherapy has its value. It is good for relieving symptoms, making people more aware of what they are doing and why, and helping them become better adjusted, which means less hostile or frightened. Often, however, it leaves people more confused and conflicted, and no more loving, than when they started.

Consider these words of a highly respected, highly experienced clinical psychologist:

> I spent my whole adult life seeking an end to my inner turmoil. I got my doctorate in psychology, but I didn't find my answers. I went into analysis and studied to be an analyst. I made progress, but the resolution was always elusive. I went into group therapy then and began experimenting to find a cure for patients and myself. I studied many new approaches, made more and more progress. I discovered Gestalt therapy and made the most dramatic progress of all. I became a Gestalt therapist myself, but still no solution. So after 18 years of practice, I came to California still looking for a resolution to my problems. . . . I've given up in despair many times and bounced back and tried again. I'm tired of just making more and more progress. I want to make it all the way.

This therapist is unusual only in his honesty in acknowledging the failure of his previous work to teach him to love and accept himself and others.

Most professional therapists know the cause of emotional problems: the programming that children receive from their parents. But *knowing is not enough.* Therapists and their clients often gain more and more knowledge without becoming any more loving because there is a split, or lack of integration, between the emotions and the intellect. More and more information into the intellect only increases the tension and conflict without really changing the program.

Another way to put this is to say that you cannot *figure* your way out of an emotional problem, you must *feel* your way out. There are therapies, which deal with the deepest feeling levels and often bring some resolution of the unfinished business from childhood. While they may go to the cause, they tend to resolve the traumas one at a time and quite slowly. The hoped-for final resolution is rare.

Therapies that don't teach self-love are never finished. They cannot be. Until your cup of love is filled to overflowing, there is always something missing in your life. No matter how well things may be going, the absence of love leaves a gaping hole in your life. Psychotherapy can and does soothe the pain around the edges and fill some of the emptiness, but those who experience it must judge for themselves whether it fills that empty space belonging to love.

While many people have searched resolutely for the secret of love, many more have not. Instead, they go through life with their eyes covered, seeing nothing. They know they hurt, and all they want is something for the pain. For them the variety of pain killers is almost endless. Food is a common way to kill the pain. When you're eating more than your body needs for nutrition and health, there is a deep reason. Beyond the infantile need for oral gratification, overeating bloats the stomach, which literally dulls the senses and dims the awareness of the outside world. While the body is working on digesting an excessive quantity of food, the intellect cannot think, and the emotions cannot be expressed, particularly the pained and angry emotions of lovelessness. The best cure for obesity, therefore, is learning to love yourself.

Like food, almost anything you take into your body, alcohol, cigarettes, and drugs of all kinds, can be used to kill the pain of not giving and receiving love. The difficulty in kicking the drinking, smoking, and drug habits is that these substances are not used for themselves but to prevent something even worse: the full experiencing of how excruciatingly painful it is to live without love. It hurts as bad as anything you can imagine. People will do anything, including killing themselves with heroin, to avoid feeling that pain. It's sad but true that what is really killing the drunks, chain smokers, and junkies is not their habits but their total lack of love for themselves and others.

Most people are more fortunate. But not much. Instead of killing themselves to avoid the pain, they live mostly anesthetized against it. They do this by using something else as a substitute for love. It is as if they say to themselves, "Well, if I can't get love from the world I'll take all the _____ I can get." You name it and people have used it as a substitute for love. Money, sex, power, fame, material possessions, whatever.

In most of the world, money and material possessions are the most widely sought after substitutes for love, in part because people equate money with one's personal value. While almost everyone agrees that money cannot buy love, almost nobody *acts* as if he believes it. Many people seem willing to settle for an unloving life if they can surround themselves with possessions. There is certainly nothing wrong with possessions in themselves. The products of human intelligence, creativity, and labor are ours to enjoy in this life, but it is a bad bargain to sacrifice love while pursuing them.

But the rich can also surround themselves with other people if they choose to, although having a lot of people around is not proof of love. Love is measured by the quality of relationships, not their quantity. In surrounding themselves with people, the rich are often lonely. There is sometimes comfort in crowds, except that in the crowd one can be lost and feel rejected. The lonely rich deserve compassion. The poor little rich boy and the poor little rich girl are just as poor in the love quotient as those in the middle class and lower class who are also without love.

Unfortunately, people continue to kid themselves that if only they had a lot of money, or a lot *more* money, they would be able to get love and feel love. An old and powerful illusion dies hard. It really is an illusion, too, since if you think about it and look at reality, you can see that people with more money are not more loving than those without it. They are undoubtedly better able to hide their pain, since they look happier and superficially may even feel better.

People can deny the truth about love and money and struggle all their lives to "prove" a lie, but the truth doesn't go away simply by denying it. What is, is. Money buys people temporarily, and it buys the substitutes for love. The real thing is beyond price.

Work is also a common substitute for love and a way of killing the pain of not getting it. People who work hard and well can even use work to acquire a lot of the other painkillers, such as money, power, and sex. If the world approves of the way they work, they can also kid themselves that the world "loves" them. The world may need the work they do—but that is economics, not love.

Work is also a way of avoiding love completely. The man

or woman who works 12 or more hours a day can use fatigue or the lack of time as excuses to avoid talking or thinking about love. For some people it is easier to be married to a business or career than to a person. It shows, too, in our divorce rates.

Weekends and vacations, too, are often filled compulsively with things to do so unloving people won't have to face how empty they feel. Travel and leisure-time industries are partially supported by the need of millions of loveless people to *do* something, *anything*, to keep from facing how bad, how thoroughly terrible, it is to live without love.

Perhaps most pathetic of all are the loners, those who live year after year with a minimum of human contact. They get up in the morning, go to their jobs, come home in the evening, eat alone, and spend the evening with a book or watching television. The next day is the same. And the next. On the weekends they go out for a walk or a drive to a museum—always alone, rarely talking to anyone, almost never touching or being touched.

Like the searching singles, loners have a variety of excuses for not making it with people: "I like my solitude." "I never found anyone I cared enough about." "It's too much trouble." "I'm hard to like." "I don't want to get involved." "They might ask something of me, and I hate to say no." And many more.

Behind the aloneness is fear. Avoiding other people, which is what loners and "independent" types are doing, is safer than risking even a temporary rebuff or rejection. As long as they're alone and don't share anything with anyone, nothing can disturb them. After a few years they find a certain level with which they can cope with a minimum of hassles, and that's it. Emotionally these people go dead for the rest of their lives.

Sartre said that hell is other people, and loners seem to live as if they believed that. Actually, hell is other people only when other people are in hell. Underneath the zombie exterior of the loners is a deep longing that is rarely acknowledged. They would love to be able to be with people, to share the big and small things of life and enjoy other people. But other people hurt them, and more importantly, they hurt themselves by continuing to remain alone.

In order to learn to love it is first necessary to know that love exists, that it is attainable, and that loving is better than not loving. For those who "know" they are unworthy of love, or who have never known love, one way to cover the pain is to deny that love exists or that it matters. Those tough people with the zombie expressions, both male and female, who rarely show any feeling beyond anger or contempt, think they are proving that love is something Madison Avenue uses to sell perfume and valentines. Or that even if love is real, nobody knows what it is. Or that even if we know what it is, love is inconvenient and a barrier to more important things.

This argument is somewhat more difficult to counter because on one level all of it is correct. Advertisers do use our intense desire for love to motivate us to buy their products. It is also accurate to say that love is difficult to define to everyone's satisfaction. Certainly it is correct that those who are involved in loving themselves and others may not spend as much time working and traveling as those who do not love. Having a more or less fixed address and an established routine does make it easier to maintain love relationships.

While all of it is accurate, none of it is true. For on a deeper level those who deny love and their need for it are attempting to "prove" a lie while protecting themselves against the pain of seeing the truth of their emptiness. Further, denying love saves risking rejection. If love doesn't exist, then you don't have to ask for it. If you don't ask, you will never be denied. It is twisted reasoning, but it makes masochistic sense.

Love is not a barrier to anything. It is the great liberator. When you love yourself for the person you are and can send that love out to others, then you have a kind of freedom unknown to those who remain uninvolved and unattached.

You can change. It is always possible to learn to love yourself and others, no matter how unloved or unloving you have been. It's never too late, and it's never too difficult. To change, though, you first need to be clear about what love is, and what it is not. Much of what looks like love is something else. In fact, people are so confused, guilty, and misinformed on the subject of love that most of them cannot even talk straight about it. Not that they don't talk about love, just that most of what they say either makes no sense or makes no difference.

For example, many people think giving is love. While it is true that lovers are givers, the reverse is not necessarily true. It all depends on the motive, and, as we have seen, there is a great difference between giving to give and giving to get. Most of the giving we see is done to get something in return. Giving money to charity, for example, is usually done in adherence to the Biblical admonition to be charitable in return for a place in heaven. Giving to get doesn't fill an empty cup of love. Perhaps you know the story of the guy who got up in church during the annual fund raising and shouted, "I wish to give $5,000 anonymously." Although he didn't say it, he could have added, "Now will you recognize me, see me, make me feel worthy, love me?" For that is really what is behind so much of charity.

This is not to condemn philanthropy, for we could not do without it. It is good for those who can afford it to help those who need it. The rich often give with good intentions. It is important, though, to demolish the myth of the virtue and unselfishness of those who give to get something in return, either real or intangible. When those who give really love themselves and others, their giving is without guilt and for no other need than that of the recipient.

Giving of ourselves also comes from various motives, many of them unloving. Self-denial and martyrdom, while serving the needs of others, is often an indirect manipulation to become one up on the other. It's as if the martyr were saying, "See how good I am at being good? Now will you love me?" Examples are all around. A recent newspaper advice column was devoted to a letter from a woman whose husband is an alcoholic. She wrote to say how much better she felt since she joined a group for wives of alcoholics. Her husband still goes out drinking every night and still makes no time for her or the children, but she's grateful to God she joined that group because now she loves him more dearly. It is OK that he does those unloving things, and they are closer than ever before. And so forth.

While this woman deserves our sympathy for her desperate situation, she is using her husband's problem to glorify herself. Secretly she is saying, "Aren't I great now? See how I put up with this awful man, and I love him, and I'm a good mother, too. I've earned some love, haven't I?"

Such martyrdom and giving to get may help explain how otherwise sensible people, both men and women, can make such one-sided marriages. They feel so worthless inside themselves that they have to "save" someone else in order to feel good about themselves. Giving to get sympathy is not love. Nor is giving to animals while ignoring people real love. As a rule, animal lovers are compassionate people, but there are many who love animals while turning away from relationships with people. Those who have been hurt often will not risk further rejection. Giving to their pets enables them to feel needed and loved.

Often what parents give to their children is not what it appears to be. Many people claim to be loving parents, offering as proof their many sacrifices on behalf of their children. While the sacrifices in time and money are easy enough to see, the expectation of something in return is usually kept hidden. Not until the children rebel or don't meet the parents' expectations does the truth come out. "How could they do this to us after all we did for them?" These anguished cries are the hallmark of parental giving to get, which is pseudo-love.

Another thing a lot of people want to prove is how sexual they are. There is probably more confusion about love and sex than any other area of life. (See Chapter 3 for a more thorough discussion of this topic.)

Many people experience strong sexual passion and mistake it for love. They get so excited around their sex object, so thoroughly exhilarated, that they're certain this is what they have been waiting for while keeping others at a distance. To him she is so perfect in every way, so exactly like the image he has carried in his head since before he can remember, it's as if his fairy godmother sent her to him. Now, he thinks, at last I have found her, and I can love freely and forever. Or anyway, for a long time. For her it's the same. He is so exciting, so strong, so manly in all the ways she has dreamed of since long ago that now she can surrender to love and give all. Well, almost all.

Sometimes they even make it together. It's exciting, it feels good, it's natural, and we live in a time of great sexual freedom and openness, so why not? No particular reason, except that while the itch in your groin is powerful, and relieving it feels good, it isn't love. Particularly if the deal is, "I'll love you and be nice to you if you'll love me and be nice to me."

Part of the confusion about love and sex comes from the odd way we have of talking about sex. We say, "I want to make love," as if it were in our power to create love. We cannot *make* love, we can only exchange the love that already exists deep within us. We also speak of "free love" as if it were just there for the taking. In loveless sex it isn't the love that is free but the body.

The confusion between sex and love also comes from the nature of the activity. The warmth and closeness of the lover's body can trigger the feeling of being at mother's breast or in father's arms with warmth and comfort. Often in sex the partners will cry out in their passion that they love each other. What they love is the moment that reminded them of the old feeling of union with mother or feeling close to father. Each is responding to his/her own nervous system that remembers mother or father and the feeling from infancy.

This is assuming, of course, that they had such physical warmth during infancy. Some children, a small but nonetheless tragic number, never feel the warmth of mother's breast or body or the strength and protection of father's arms. Without this important childhood experience of physical, emotional, and spiritual closeness it is almost impossible to experience, much less enjoy, adult sexuality. Or adult love. Those who were not handled with tenderness as children find it all but impossible to express or receive tenderness as adults. Fortunately, total lack of physical handling is rare. What most of us missed is the consistent experience of emotional tenderness.

This restimulation of childhood feelings during sexual intercourse helps explain how lovers can be so passionate in bed and so cold and unloving afterward. It isn't necessarily that they dislike each other except for sex. Rather, who the other person actually is doesn't matter since he/she is just a stand-in for mother or father.

What, then, happened to love? The answer is that as children we did not learn how to love. Instead, we saw our parents kidding themselves that the substitutes they accepted in place of love were the real thing. Instead of seeing the truth we saw the lie and believed it. Thus, we learned to think love is sex, money, food, martyrdom, hard work, or poetry.

Love is a feeling and a state of being, and it comes from the spiritual essence within ourselves. We learn to feel it by experiencing it directly in our relations with our parents during our childhood. If we experience more than enough love during those formative years, there will be a lifelong surplus we can share with others. If we don't learn to love during childhood, the things we do as adults that look like love are just play-acting, and if all we know how to do is act love, we are in for a great deal of emptiness and pain.

Love between men and women is particularly susceptible to the danger of acting a part. Romance and sexual encounters are so much a part of popular entertainment that what most people know about love, or think they know, comes from television, movies, and books. The tragedy is that most of what is dramatic in popular love stories is not love but various kinds of manipulation. Since heartache and catastrophe are more familiar than quiet happiness, the stories most people associate with love are filled with frustration, conflict, and corruption.

There are several important conclusions to be drawn from all of this. First, you cannot figure your way out of your failure to love yourself. Lack of self-love is like a locked cage, and intellect is not the key. You cannot just get a book full of good ideas, pay real close attention, stop doing all those bad things while practicing all the good things, and emerge several months later from your room a full-fledged lover. (You may even have picked up this book with something like that in mind.) Books cannot teach people how to love, although they are helpful in giving information and understanding. If books could teach love and how to feel it, we might have stopped with the Old Testament, which contains a great deal of wisdom, entertainment, and beautiful writing.

It may seem odd using a book to tell you a book cannot make you into a lover. Yet this is the easiest way to share information with a large number of people. Although *knowing* won't solve an emotional problem, knowing that you don't know is the beginning of true knowledge.

Second, there are no tricks to the truth of self-love. Meditation, psychoanalysis, jogging, drugs, encounter, fasting, massage, you name it, none of them will make any difference in your love life until you learn to love yourself.

Third, and best of all, there *is* a way out. Despite the negativity of much of what I have said, there is hope for everyone. You *can* learn to love yourself. Change is possible for anyone, but not solely through admonitions, prayer, psychologizing, or reading books. No matter how stuck you may feel, no matter how negative your life is or has been, what you have always hoped for yourself really is possible.

While this book cannot make it happen for you, it can show

you how things went wrong and what others have done to make them right again. When they are right, you will be able freely and constructively to exchange the love that is at the base of your deepest longings. You will love, not because someone told you to, but because deep inside you *are* a lover. Everyone is. It is there, and it is available, no matter how long or how deeply it has been hidden. Like a diamond, love can be buried but not destroyed.

Showing is not doing. This book shows the origin of our inability to love ourselves and recounts what is still, to me, the incredible story of how I was taught to teach others how to love themselves. Take what you can from this book while recognizing that love is more than something to read about. Once learned, it is the ultimate human experience.

2. How Children Adopt Their Parents

Kids have it rough. Whether rich or poor, in large families or small, all children live in a world they did not create, run by rules they did not make. From their point of view their lives are controlled by big, powerful people who are often inconsistent, illogical, hypocritical, frightening, cold and, in some cases, even brutal and violent.

Children experience the unpredictability of mother's and father's love. They feel as if they are always on probation, always having to prove themselves. Before parents teach them not to recognize it, children are also aware of the difference between the real love they need and the play-acting that often substitutes for the real thing. Almost no child has the parents he or she deserves.

These are hard truths to confront. However clearly we see the flaws in our parents, we nonetheless cling to the belief that they loved us. Many people know they are still angry over some of the things their parents did, but they have achieved some compassion and understanding for them. Many of us also realize that if we had it tough as kids, our parents may have had it even tougher when they were children. We therefore tend to cherish our good childhood memories while trying to forgive and forget the bad. Nevertheless, it is only by seeing the entire truth about our parents that we can establish a basis for true compassion and love for them.

Most parents do not deliberately mistreat or harm their children. In the adult world we do the best we can in the face of our human failings and the stresses of making our way in life. Almost everyone knows that he or she has good days, bad days, and an occasional day that is best forgotten. As adults we struggle to learn to live with these ups and downs of ourselves and others.

Children live in a different world. Children have no choice but to believe that their parents and other adults always know what they are doing. Adults own and run the world, don't they? Therefore, in whatever way a child sees his parents treating him, he assumes it is intentional and right, which can be confusing. After all, how can these people who (usually) say they love him, intentionally treat him so harshly and unlovingly? Most children at one time or another have said to themselves something like, "They say they love me but . . ."

If you are like most people, you can remember times in your first five years when you were punished unjustly or excessively, and you retreated to a private place to nurse your hurt or angry feelings. Perhaps, while crying bitter tears, you decided that these people you lived with were not your real parents. You may even have had a fantasy explanation for the inconsistency. A mix-up at the hospital, perhaps. Or maybe when your parents went on vacation, they were kidnaped, their bodies taken over by beings from outer space. (Children are imaginative.) Many children also think they have been adopted and that someday their real parents will return to claim (or rescue) them and give them the love and protection they yearn for and know are rightfully theirs. Some children will even ask if they are adopted, much to the consternation or amusement of their parents. People have told me they secretly went looking for their adoption papers in their parents' closets and drawers.

In fact, the overwhelming reality of our emotional lives is exactly the opposite. It is *we* who adopt our parents. We attempt to be like our parents, and in so doing we adopt their positive and negative traits in return for both their positive and negative attention. Little boys try to strut like their fathers; little girls try to sit like their mothers. Almost every child at some time or other says or thinks, "I'm going to be like Daddy (or Mommy) when I grow up."

Parents even tend to encourage the imitation by laughing approvingly at a child's attempts to be grown-up. They enjoy it if the aping is positive. Sometimes they even enjoy it when it's negative. When children are playing house, for example, if the little girl scolds the "late" little boy the way mother scolds father when he's late for dinner, and the little boy imitates father's sheepish withdrawal behind the newspaper, the parents may laugh at the recognition of a common household drama.

But if it is funny to the parents, it is deadly serious to a child. He imitates them and adopts their traits to get their love and approval, which he desperately needs to sustain himself. This pattern is so common that we have a number of sayings in English that reflect it: "Like father, like son," "The apple doesn't fall far from the tree," and so forth. Behind these sayings is often the mistaken assumption that children inherit their emotional similarity to their parents. On the contrary, children become like their parents by adopting the traits they see in daily life. Children react positively or negatively to the actions of those in charge of them. Negative reactions cause neurotic behavior patterns.

Children adopt both the positive qualities that please their parents and the negative qualities that annoy them. Adopting their negative traits is where the real problems begin. If mother is fearful, for example, the child learns not to take risks. Or if father is unemotional, the child learns not to show his feelings. When mother doesn't think much, the child learns not to solve problems. When father is a procrastinator, the child learns to be late most of the time. If mother and father each have the same negative trait, then the child gets a double dose of negativity.

Everyone has some positivity, no matter how negatively he or she behaves. We aren't dwelling here on positivity because this is a book about problems, and the positive traits are not a problem for people unless they rebel against them.

The most negative trait possible is the inability to love oneself and others. If our parents did not know how to love themselves and others, they could not teach us how to give and receive love. Our parents' failure to teach us to love ourselves and others (including even them!) is the emotional cancer in our lives. Almost the entire catalogue of human misery and misfortune can be traced directly or indirectly to this "disease." If lovelessness can be likened to a cancer, then the "virus" that causes it is *negative love.* (Although I coined this expression in 1967, the concept has been known but largely ignored for many years.)

The negative love pattern is the key to all neurotic, negative behavior patterns, especially the inability to love. When one adopts the negative traits, moods, or admonitions (silent or overt) of either or both parents, one relates to them with negative love. It is illogical logic, nonsensical sense, and insane sanity, yet the pursuit of the love they never received in childhood is the reason people persist in behaving in these destructive patterns.

Although adopting our parents' negative traits affects our ability to love, it is not limited to that one area of life. The adoption includes literally hundreds of traits, both important and trivial, covering every facet of our being. The negative love pattern is the single most destructive force in marriage, sexuality, work, health, and happiness. There is no area of our lives that is unaffected by the example our parents set for us and the way we continue to be affected by it.

You can see this for yourself in your own life. Take a moment to sit back and relax. Recall your mother during your childhood. Picture her in a familiar room, perhaps the living room or the kitchen. See her doing or saying something typical that particularly annoyed you. Perhaps she nagged about insignificant things or was stingy with praise. It need not be something she did with you, although it may be. The point is to see something about her that was negative. (You do know your parents weren't perfect, don't you?) Take a moment now to visualize one or two other scenes of your mother doing or saying something that you did not like when you were a child. It often helps to close your eyes while doing this. Experience it now.

After seeing a few of mother's negative traits, do the same with your father. See him doing or saying something characteristic of him that made you unhappy or uncomfortable when you were a child. For example, he may have disciplined you harshly or unfairly, or showed no interest in the things that mattered to you. If you have difficulty seeing anything negative about your father or your mother, remember that even the best parents are not without some negative qualities. When you have seen two or three negative traits for each parent, (or their surrogates*), make a note of them.

Now take a gentle but honest look at yourself. How do your father's and mother's negative qualities express themselves in you? Have you become like them? Are their flaws now *your* flaws? If your mother nagged and carped at others over little things, do you do it, too? Do you have the same difficulty she had in complimenting others when they do a good job? Are you like your father in overreacting to other people's failings or mistakes? Do you have little enthusiasm for the things that excite others, just like your father? Whatever their negativities, your parents are now part of you. You may even find these traits as annoying now as you did then and perhaps wonder why you are exhibiting in yourself the patterns and traits that you disliked in your parents.

If you have difficulty deciding what you have done with the trait you disliked in your mother or father, consider asking someone who knows you well and can be objective about you. Most people need some help seeing the things about themselves they dislike.

Not only do we adopt both the positive and negative traits of our parents, we do it for the same extremely important reason: We want their love and approval. To a child, becoming like his mother and father appears to be the way to gain that love. However, if mother and father do not know how to give and receive selfless love, it won't work for the child. Imitating them will not gain him real love, only its pale substitutes. For example, if mother is meddlesome and pushy, she probably won't respond lovingly when she is on the receiving end of this trait from her own child. Parents may want their children to become like them, but they don't enjoy having their own negativities mirrored back to them. Instead of positive, loving attention, which feels good, the child will receive negative attention, which hurts. When his parents punish him for doing what they do, he may, with justification, say, "But that's what *you* do, Mommy." Or, "But Daddy, *you* do it." This tends to incite the parents even more, for they then become angry with the child and angry with themselves. The child may wind up with a double dose of anger for mirroring his parents, while getting

*If your natural parents didn't raise you, then substitute the person or persons who assumed parental responsibility for you.

lost in confusion: "How come it's all right for Mommy and Daddy, and it's not all right for me?" When a child is chastised for doing what his parents do, the result is tremendous insecurity and instability.

Worse still, if mother and father do not know how to love themselves and others, they cannot give the positive trait of love as a model for their children to adopt. Instead, they show the negative trait of self-criticism and condemnation, which children then adopt along with all the other negative traits they see, hear, and feel.

Furthermore, if father and mother did not really love *each other,* then their children will also adopt the negative trait of not loving others. This is the real problem for almost everyone. We pursue the love they did not know how to give and become unloving as part of that quest for love.

When I was growing up, the word "love" was never used in our home. It was almost like a dirty word. My mother would say, "What is love? It doesn't exist." I learned to believe that in my early years. It took me many years before I could even say the word, much less understand it and give it meaning. Love didn't exist for my mother, so for many years it didn't exist for me.

To see this in your own life, again recall your mother. How was her love life? Did she have warm, loving people around her? Was she able to exchange love freely with persons of both sexes? Did she have the kind of sex life she deeply wanted? Did she love herself and give to herself as well as to others? If she is still alive, what is her love life like right now?

Now do the same with your father. How was his love life? Did people know him well and love him? Did he get to know others well and love them in return? Did he have the kind of sex life he deeply wanted? Did he love himself and treat himself as well as he treated others? If he is still alive, what is his love life like right now?

After looking closely at your parents and their love life, compare it with your own. If you are like most people, your love life is not much different from that of your parents. (Or perhaps your love life is different from your parents', and it is taking a great deal of effort and energy to pretend to be the loving person your parents were not.) The point is that the quality of your love life is no coincidence. You learned, or more likely did not learn, how to love yourself and others by following your parents' example. The inability to love oneself and others is the most negative trait there is. Those who do not love have adopted this negative trait from their parents in exchange for pseudo-love, which is acting a part rather than having a genuine feeling. It may hurt us and make poor sense, but almost no child dares rise above the level of his parents.

Thus, "Whatever happened to love?" is that it was corrupted by your parents. Whether they did it intentionally or unintentionally is another matter. Their intentions don't change the facts. If your mother and father did not know how to love themselves and others, they could not teach love to you.

Some people will have no trouble understanding this since they already know how cold and unloving their parents were. If your father got drunk and beat the hell out of you and your mother, you already know that he didn't love you. Other people, though, may be offended because they feel their parents were good, loving people. Still others may refuse to believe their parents could have done them any harm. I agree that most parents mean only well for their children. Yet once people take off the blinders their parents put on them, they discover that their childhood was not as loving as they think and that their parents, no matter how well-meaning, were quite unkind and hurtful in many ways.

Again, take a clear look at your love life. If your parents were the good, loving people you say, then why aren't you totally loving of yourself and others? How is it that you failed to learn the lesson of love they offered you? What we become is no accident. If we didn't learn love, it is because they didn't know how to teach it.

Here, for example, is an excerpt from the writing of a young man beginning to see clearly his negative love relationship with his father and its continuing impact on his love life:

> I was afraid of his anger, awed by his pseudo-power, and emulated him in every way possible. He quickly learned the effectiveness of the power he had over me and would use that power to discipline me by saying something like, "If you want to be a man like Dad, you'll have to do it this way." He was concerned that I should meet his expectations when we were together around people. If he was

pleased with me, he would call me "Bud," which was short for "Buddy." If he was displeased, he would call me "Jim" and make some connection between my actions and my mother's personality. I would do anything within my power to sustain the "Bud" level of communication with him. . . . He would suggest to me that he knew that it was difficult to relate to women because they were inferior, but that I should placate them (my mother and sisters), as that would make conditions easier for both him and me, while at the same time it would satisfy the "silly" women. . . . Now I find myself distrusting women and putting them down, and I can't maintain a relationship. . . . I'm only comfortable in the presence of other men, but even then I'm not happy. I'm cold and confused and lonely. I don't know who I am or what to believe . . . and I don't even know how to smile. I'm as joyless and wooden as he was!

Jim certainly became the "Buddy" his father wanted him to be. Girls, too, become the women their mothers show them. A young woman named Jean wrote the following in describing the constant battle between her mother and her father:

"My mother treated my father with blatant disrespect. Her resentment was very open . . . she would insult him and make fun of him in public, accusing him of being lazy. My father would insult back, threaten to leave her and drink."

During the course of her work with me she wrote a distraught letter concerning her current problems with her husband: "My husband and I are arguing over my wanting him to work more and his wanting me to stay home and clean house. He is also threatening to leave me because I am too outspoken and not submissive enough."

These two anguished people are each relating to their parents, (Jim to his father, Jean to her mother), with total negative love. Each is perfectly emulating the trait from the parent of the same sex, becoming "father's little boy" and "mother's little girl." It does not lead to a happy life, but children have little choice. When they don't get the real love and acceptance they need, they find it necessary to *do something* to gain mother's or father's attention or pseudo-love. When genuine love isn't available, children have to settle for false, negative love. Then at least mother and father know they exist.

The interaction between parents and children is hardly this simple, of course. Children adopt negative traits from both parents without becoming a carbon copy of either one. In many areas they rebel and do the opposite of what mother and father want. The freewheeling, hell-raising daughter of the pious minister is a classic example of a child rebelling against parental example. Yet, however successful the rebellion may be on the surface, it is not what it appears to be. Inside this kind of rebellious person there is usually deep remorse and inner frustration over the failure of the rebellion to substitute for the real love she never got from her father. Rebellion always leads to conflict.

Rebellion also shows itself in less serious ways. A woman client was once telling me that she was a good housekeeper like her mother. Since I knew the client to be quite rebellious, I probed a little.

"You mean every room in your house is neat?" I asked. "All your drawers, too?"

"Yes," she said. "Every room." She paused and then said, "Except the sewing room. That's always a mess. But that's just my sewing room."

"Nonsense," I said. "You may think you're doing it mother's way, but you're allowing yourself a space to be sloppy, which is rebellion against your mother's neatness. You must be frustrated and in conflict."

She thought about it a moment and then said, "You know, you're right, Bob. I always feel uncomfortable with the way that room looks. I guess I do have a conflict over her neatness."

Children rebel against their parents because they are angry with them. Every rebellious child is raging inside over his parents' failure to show him the love he desperately needs and wants. What they are angry about is that they don't *feel* loved despite the loving words they may hear. Since it is usually unsafe and often ineffective for a child to express his anger directly, the anger takes on disguises. Instead of screaming, "No! You can't make me!" the angry child learns to "get even" by doing poorly in school, ignoring the rules at home, or in some other way. Secretly the angry, emotional child is saying, "Nyaah, nyaah. I'll show you, bad mother and father. You want me to do it your way, but I won't. *You'll* be sorry." Many of the self-destructive problems of adulthood can be traced to the rebellion of a child who is still angry with mother and father.

Frequently a child is angry, for example, over the competition with his brothers and sisters for the attention and approval of mother and father. Children often learn early that there is not enough love to go around. If an older brother gets positive attention for being highly intelligent and a good student, the younger one may decide he cannot compete with his brother and will rebel by pretending to be stupid and lazy. By rebelling in this destructive way he gains the negative attention of one or both parents. If this sounds masochistic and illogical, it is. Positive love makes more sense and feels better than negative love and negative attention. When a child sees that only negative attention is available from his parents, he will choose it over no attention at all.

Rebellion always leads to inner conflict, which results in the seesaw feeling we experience when there are competing messages inside our heads. Ask yourself how often you have told yourself you need to do a particular thing in order to enhance your life. And you really intend to do it, and you know it's right. Yet you wind up doing just the opposite while feeling uncomfortable over your failure to change. This emotional conflict also shows itself when you sometimes do things one way and other times another, never really feeling good about either. In many ways our toughest problems come when we're struggling in conflict as a result of rebelling against our parents, for all inner conflict stems from the negative love created in parental relationships.

Conflict has several different sources. If a child receives competing messages from mother and father, he may be torn apart trying to please both. For example, if father is a spendthrift and mother hates to spend money, the child is doomed to lose either way. If he expresses negative love for father by spending wildly, he will be rebelling against mother, causing conflict. If he saves his money, expressing negative love for mother, he will be rebelling against father's trait, causing another conflict. He may buy the most expensive equipment for his hobby while eating only in the cheapest restaurants he can find. By doing both he relates to both parents in the pattern of negative love.

There is a subtle irony in this example. Father's spending and mother's saving may balance the marriage financially.

However, what may be a workable arrangement for a husband and wife can be a hidden but agonizing source of conflict and guilt for their children.

Conflict also arises from competing messages in the intellect and the emotions. The rebellious emotional child within may be doing something the intellect knows is dangerous or destructive. Such destructive behaviors as cigarette smoking, alcoholism, overeating, and drug addiction are common sources of conflict. Our intellects tell most of us that these things are damaging and life threatening, yet the rebellious child within says something like, "Try and stop me, Mother! I'll show *you.*" (This conflict between the intellect and the emotions is the reason most attempts to solve addictive, problem behaviors are ineffective. No amount of information or encouragement is powerful enough to counter the force of the angry, rebellious child underneath the veneer of intellect. In the most extreme cases even the fear of untimely death is not strong enough.)

Jane was the child of a handsome, sadistic father and a pretty, masochistic mother. During her childhood the only attention she received from him was an almost daily beating. While hitting her, he would scream, "Take that! Take that! Take that!" In terror and pain she would cry, "Don't, Daddy! Don't, Daddy! Don't!" Since any attention is better than being ignored, she masochistically learned to love the negative attention she was getting from Daddy. The hidden emotional justification was, "At least Daddy sees me. I have contact with him." During her childhood years the only physical touching between them were these painful, humiliating beatings. She also saw him beat her mother.

With the mother and father she had, it was almost inevitable that as an adult she would express her negative love for them by marrying a handsome man who, like her father, was a sadist. Whenever her husband beat her, the negative emotional child within her silently cried out to her father, "See, Daddy? I'm not being disloyal to you. The man I married is beating me up just like you did me and Mommy. Now will you love me, Daddy?"

And from deep within she plaintively cried out to her mother, "Mommy, I didn't outdo you. My man's beating me up just the way Daddy beat you up. I'm not disloyal to you and your values. I'm just the same as you. I haven't risen above you. Now will you love me, Mommy, and feel sorry for me?"

The power behind this pathetic pattern was her childhood fear that in outdoing her parents she would not be loyal to them and thus become unworthy of their love. Finally, however, she did rebel and divorce her sadist husband.

For her second husband she chose a kind, thoughtful, loving man. While this looked like a successful rebellion, it was not. He was a good husband to her, yet she was miserable. She would sob to me, "He is so good, Bob, but I can't love him." She had dared to rebel against Daddy and was paying the price for it. She had gone into a frustrating conflict between negative love for her father and her attempt to rebel against him. The negative child within, to defend itself against the rebellious act, cried out to her parents, "See, Daddy, I'm still loyal to you because I'm not really loving this good man even though I rebelled and married him. I haven't totally deserted you, Daddy. And, Mommy, I haven't outdone you. I rebelled, Mommy, but I'm not letting him love me. So I'm not getting any more love than you did. Now will you love me?"

The story of Jane's unhappy marriages, although somewhat extreme, shows several important aspects of negative love and its variants, rebellion and conflict. Her destructive negative love for her father and mother remained with her into adulthood and determined her choice of a husband. Second, while her intellect may have known that the first husband was a poor choice, the negative emotional child was the part of her that made the decision. Her negative emotional child was also in control during her second marriage. While her situation may have improved on the surface, it was not much better on the emotional level. Third, her conflict was what prevented her from accepting the love her intellect knew was available in the second marriage. Her negative love patterns were so powerful she was unable to break them by herself.

Jane received her negative love patterns from both parents. The lack of one parent does not necessarily simplify or ease the situation. A missing parent has an enormous influence, as the story of Ellen shows. Her father deserted her and her mother when she was 4 years old. Her mother spent the next 40 years alone and lonely, rejecting any possibility of male friendship, companionship, or love.

Ellen blamed her mother for her father's flight and became

bitterly hostile and angry. She spent her adult life in shallow, brief marriages with a succession of men from whom she wanted to get the love her missing father took with him. When single, she was desperate to be married, which was rebellion against her mother. Yet shortly after each wedding she began to find fault with the current relationship. She would not allow any man to give her the love her father did not give her. Stuck as she was in the resulting conflict, she was miserable when she was married and miserable when she was divorced. She clung to each marriage until she could stand it no longer and then would leave. Finally, in her fifties, she ceased her rebellion and recognized that she could not be content in a loving relationship with a man, which would have been outdoing mother. Worn out by the conflict resulting from rebelling against her mother, she gave up and settled for spending the rest of her life alone, just like mother.

Like many people with emotional problems, Jane and Ellen were unaware of how their troubles stemmed from negative love patterns. In their ignorance they sincerely believed their acts of rebellion would bring them greater happiness and love. It is this common but mistaken belief that one's acts of rebellion will lead to something better that adds poignancy to the tragedy of the negative love relationship with parents.

Besides their traits and moods, children also adopt their parents' negative admonitions, both spoken and unspoken. "You're not good enough" is so frequent an admonition it is almost universal. Children who live with criticism stand little chance of learning to love themselves. A 45-year-old doctor, highly competent and respected in his profession, recalled this childhood scene as one of many examples of his mother's devastating criticism:

> I was not quite five years old. I asked my mother if I could put stamps on her letters. I put them on crooked —I'd seen mail come to the house with stamps on crooked and thought that was the way people put stamps on letters. Later, she saw the letters with crooked stamps and exploded into anger. "Why didn't you put them on straight? They look terrible. I'm ashamed to send them out. You're a bad boy! Naughty!" I felt crushed. I thought I was doing the right thing, but

> she acted like I was stupid and had done a bad thing on purpose. My stomach felt tight and hurt.

While this man followed his parents' desires in becoming a doctor, he also adopted his mother's negative admonitions. He was bright and hard-working, yet he carried into adulthood the terrible doubts about his competence instilled by his mother's frequent criticisms. In medical school he nervously crammed for examinations even when he was thoroughly prepared. In his later medical practice he often called in specialists to confirm diagnoses he already knew were correct. He never learned to trust himself because he was consumed with the self-doubt he had learned from his mother.

Besides the obvious spoken admonitions, parents also give their children powerful silent admonitions. Usually the silent admonition comes as the companion to a more innocent spoken one. For example, the spoken admonition, "Mind your manners," carries with it the unstated implication, "Your manners are not good," or "If I don't remind you all the time, you'll forget." Kids get the real message even when nothing is said.

Here is how a 40-year-old minister described one of his childhood experiences with the silent admonition not to express warmth physically: "I remember going to bed at night when I was about seven. I wanted her to come in and hug me good night, but she'd only come as far as the door and say, 'Good night. Don't forget to say your prayers,' as she turned out the light. I'd lay there hating her and plotting ways to get even because she didn't care enough to come in and give me a hug!"

Although his mother may not have realized it, she was teaching her son something more influential in his life than just to say his prayers at night. He adopted both her spoken admonition to pray and the even more powerful silent admonition not to touch those who were dear to him. As a parent himself, he found it impossible to embrace his children, and they were learning from him the same lesson he learned from his mother.

Not all admonitions are given or received so quietly as were those of the minister's mother. Sometimes they are part of harsh disciplining. A 28-year-old salesman told me of such an incident from when he was 4 years old:

My mother was standing at the front door talking to the mailman and I was playing on the floor. I was directly underneath her and looked up, curiously, under her dress. This so enraged her that she immediately pulled me up and slapped and scolded me in front of this stranger. The pain and embarrassment and guilt were so great that it most surely laid a foundation for my unease with women and sex.

So deeply did this man take into himself the admonition that it is wicked to look at a woman's body, that after ten years of marriage he still cannot bring himself to watch his wife undress. He knows intellectually that there is nothing wrong with seeing her naked and that it ought to please and excite him. But his emotional programming overwhelms his present-day knowledge, and he responds to the sight of his wife's body with the fear and shame his mother drove into him.

Acts of omission during childhood create as many problems as acts of commission. The things parents do not do and do not say are equally effective in programming the child. For example, if a child does not see his father demonstrating love and affection for his mother, and does not see mother asking for it, he will learn not to be demonstrative. Later, in adult life, when he is expected to show love he may find the best he can do is play a role. This sort of pretending is especially common in love and sexual relations. People who have not learned to feel love for others are expected to act as if they did. Books and movies are often used to teach people how to play the part of a lover without actually feeling it. If love affairs, marriages, even friendships, have an empty and incomplete feeling to them, it is often because there is little or no genuinely warm feeling below the surface action. To be real, love must be learned in childhood.

Another common act of omission that has severely damaging consequences is simply for the parents to be unavailable for the child. When the parents are usually so busy with their own interests and activities that the child feels they do not really see or hear him, he learns to adopt the belief, "I don't matter to others." A divorced mother who adopted this admonition recalled this scene as typical of her childhood:

When I was two, I toddled up to my mother and tugged at her skirt to get her attention. She brushed me away, saying that she was busy. I always remember her as busy. I remember her rushing around pell-mell at breakneck speed, with millions of little errands and chores she felt she had to do. The mornings were a total rush. She wanted everyone dressed and fed in the narrow time limits she kept. She was always anxious that her time plan wouldn't be kept—that one of the kids would do something spontaneous and she wouldn't get everything done in just the way she wanted.

From her busy mother she learned to be a busy, harried mother herself. She, too, is running around, keeping schedules and being short-tempered with her children while getting angry with herself because she is behaving like her mother. She is also frustrated because she doesn't know what to do about it. The heavy demands on her time and energy in running a household with no husband are compounded tragically by her emotional need to emulate her mother.

In addition to the effect of acts of omission, it is important to realize that the negative love programming need not include severe trauma or family uproar. A quiet household is not necessarily a loving one. In fact, children of parents who fought often find it easier to express their feelings than children of those who kept a false peace. The programming and adopting of their traits, moods, and admonitions goes on day after day, quietly, in many cases with little or no awareness of what is happening. Often it isn't until people compare their childhood recollections with others that they consciously realize how many important things were missing from their home life.

To summarize, children adopt their parents' negativities in return for pseudo-love, which serves as an inadequate substitute for real love. When children rebel against their parents, they experience conflict and anxiety, which block the natural flow of love. The almost universal failure to love is the most destructive adopted negative love pattern.

This is the basic structure of the negative love concept, but in life it is even more complex than so far described. Children of the same parents do not turn out the same. Brothers and sisters, even twins, are quite individualistic and diverse. There are several reasons for this. The family changes as time passes. New parents with only one child are different from the parents they become after a second or third child. Also, as the family changes, the situation facing each new child alters, the amount depending on how much the family itself has changed. There is a great difference between a three-person household consisting of mother, father, and 3-year-old, and a four-person household consisting of the same mother, no father, and three children ages 8, 5, and 2. Thus, the negative love programming of each child can change during the years from embryo to puberty, and the programming of all the children is rarely as similar as it seems.

On the other hand, even when the programming changes little from one child to the next, children who are close in age do not usually respond to it in the same way. The pattern of the older, goody-goody child and the younger, rebellious child is a common one. Each child experiences basically the same set of traits, moods, and admonitions from mother and father, yet they respond differently. If the older child so closely fits the parents' expectations that he receives large amounts of positive attention from both mother and father, the younger may view the three as an unbreakable triangle. If no more positive attention appears to be available, the usual recourse is to rebel and gain the parents' negative attention. The first child is responding to the programming with total negative love, while the second is responding with rebellion. On the other hand, if the older son feels displaced by the younger, to whom mother and father are giving all the positive attention, the older may be the one to rebel.

Even when children respond to the programming in the same basic manner, that is, compliance or rebellion, the response can take different forms. Children don't necessarily rebel in the same way. Consider the case of John and his two sons, John, Jr., and Peter. In the 1940s and early 1950s John was a dedicated Communist, which by then was not only unfashionable but dangerously illegal. To his associates in the party he seemed a strong, loving man who was always talking, organizing, conspiring, and pouring his energy into the movement for the social change he was convinced was vital to the welfare of the entire world. Meanwhile, his family lived in poverty and saw little of him since everything beyond necessities went for the benefit of his cause.

In his later years John became deeply disillusioned about the possibility of social change. As a result he suffered from devastating insomnia and took heavier and heavier doses of sleeping pills to control it. Eventually his health failed, and he died of a drug overdose. John, Jr., was 12, Peter was 10 when their father died.

How each responded to the programming of their father reveals the subtle complexity of negative love and its variants, rebellion and conflict. Both rebelled by taking no interest in politics or the welfare of others. John, Jr., rebelled against his father's poverty and concern for the "oppressed workers" and strove compulsively to join the Capitalist financiers against whom his father fought. Ignoring his wife and children, he became obsessed with making money. While it appeared he would achieve his financial goal, the conflict he experienced because of his rebellion, and the destruction of his family life, left him suffering from nervous anxiety, which kept him awake night after night.

Peter, too, rebelled against his father's social example. However, he adopted his father's drug dependency, and even became a dealer in heroin. Because of his conflict over his rebellion, he avoided succeeding by being careless at the wrong times, and spent several years in jail.

As children, Peter and John, Jr., admired their dedicated father but hated him for destroying himself and abandoning them. In their anger and frustration, they each rebelled against his social concern and pseudo-love of others by pursuing purely selfish goals, although in radically different styles—but emotionally they were each stuck in rebellion and conflict.

With negative love, nothing is quite as it seems to be. The so-called ideal child, for example, can be the delight of his parents for a while. Often a perfectly compliant child will "go crazy" with rebellion as he enters puberty. While it is tempting for parents to dismiss it as "a phase he's going through" or the result of hormonal changes, there is often much more involved. The ideal child is buying mother's and father's love, but the pressure he feels is overwhelming. He experiences the frustration of always doing things their way while never receiving the real love that is the promised reward for being "good." As his contact with the outside world increases, he becomes aware that others live without having to meet the impossible expectations he faces at home. A child understands justice even if he doesn't see it at home, and the idea that others are "getting away with it" while he isn't can produce overpowering rage and pain.

It may take longer than the first 13 years for the pressure to burst. If the pressure builds more slowly, or the "child" has more stamina to withstand it, the upheaval may not come until the late thirties or early forties. Sooner or later there comes a time for most people when they no longer will compliantly feed negative love nickels into mother's and father's slot machine, especially if the "jackpot" never comes or the infrequent payoff is in wooden nickels of pseudo-love.

Many people find much or all of what I am saying unbelievable or offensive. Those who voice their objections often say something like, "What you're saying may apply to certain kinds of unfortunate, low-life people, but it doesn't apply to me. My parents were deeply in love with each other, and they were wonderful to us children. They were happy all their married lives and raised a beautiful family."

Maybe so. After all, there is a fortunate small minority of the world who do know how to love themselves and others selflessly and without any hang ups. Maybe your parents were part of that small group. If so, you are correct that this doesn't apply to you. One way to test this, however, is to see how *you* turned out. If your parents were really among those who love truly, they would have been able to fill your cup of love and send you into the world prepared to share that love with others. Which brings us back to the key question: How's your love life? If your love life isn't as "perfect" as that of your parents, what went wrong? Either they did or did not teach you how to create and maintain a satisfactory love life. One simply cannot live day after day for the first thirteen years of life experiencing a loving relationship between one's parents and then "somehow" fail to learn how to do the same for oneself. That idea doesn't make sense.

At the same time I can't accept the argument that loving parents sometimes produce an unloving child. For a number of reasons children often don't see clearly what is going on between their parents. If mother and father are each living under their own negative love admonitions to keep the peace by not showing their angry or hurt feelings, particularly at home, the pseudo-love at the dinner table may actually fool the children. This sort of charade is particularly successful if the children also receive a negative love admonition to invalidate their own perceptions and intuitions. The children may end up confused and guilty over their inability as adults to love the way they thought mother and father did. At the same time, mother and father may wonder themselves how the kids could have "gone wrong."

A common kind of false loving marriage is one between a father-type husband and a daughter-type wife, who come together and are compatible because of their complementary dependency needs. It can survive as long as Big Daddy takes care of his Little Girl, and neither of them wants to change it. While this may be a "workable" arrangement, it is not a mature love between two adults, which is what children need to see and experience in order to achieve it in their own adulthood.

There are seemingly loving marriages that nonetheless produce children who cannot love. If mother's and father's love for each other is inflexible and exclusive, there may be no room for a child to join them. If the child sees his mother and father giving love to each other while ignoring him, he may walk away and reject them because he himself feels rejected. Later, the parents may wonder why he won't respond when they want to give him love. It is because they didn't spread out their love to include him in its protective, comforting warmth. No matter what is going on between the parents, if the circle of love isn't open to their children, the next generation will have no love of their own for themselves or others.

A child may also learn to be unloving if his father sees him as competition for the love and attention of his mother. If this immature father sends his child the silent admonition, "Get lost, kid," the child may have no choice but to withdraw, which expresses his negative love for Daddy. Further, if mother's silent admonition is the opposite, "Don't leave me," the child may bounce back and forth like a football. No matter which admonition he adopts, he will find himself in rebellion against one of his parents, thus leading to constant, debilitating conflict.

Both rebellion and the resulting conflict originate in the

negative love patterns. Some people, though, have difficulty accepting my choice of words. "How can love be negative?" they ask. "Love just is. What you describe is certainly negative, but it isn't love."

When you emulate mother's and father's positive qualities because you admire and love them and want to be like them, the result is positive. (If mother and father were charitable, for example, they may have taught you the positive trait of giving lovingly in order to give.) On the other hand, when people emulate the bad traits of mother and father in attempting to gain their "love," the result is the spectrum of human misery, degradation, and destruction. Our innate, diamondlike love is then covered with the negative traits and patterns of mother and father. The "crud" on top of your diamond is this negativity you adopted.

The case of an unrequited love also shows the positive and negative aspects of love. When the positive love we feel for another is not returned, we hurt with the pain of rejection and misery. (Some people have said of this kind of love, "It hurts real good.") While the feeling of love is overwhelmingly beautiful when you want to give it to someone, it is also overwhelmingly devastating when not returned. Often people don't want to be positively loved and accepted, although they may not fully know this. Many people feel that love is too good for them, without realizing that if their love relationships are better than their parents' were they will be outdoing them. One of the most powerful of the parental silent admonitions is, "Don't outdo me."

Some people argue with the idea of negative love by asserting that each of us has free will and that we have no one to blame for our troubles but ourselves. Yet, though we tell ourselves we have free will and control over our destinies, for most of us most of the time, autonomy is an illusion. Instead, what we do is replay the programming laid down for us by our parents during our childhood. Those who insist on their own autonomy should be aware that an important part of the program is to be unaware that it is a program. Parents tell their children the lie that they are free agents and then order them to believe it.

Some people who wish to avoid looking at themselves put the blame for their negativity on the "unconscious," as if it were an ugly black bucket of demons and evil that comes with them as part of their equipment at birth and over which they have no control or understanding.

We begin life pure. Everything that influences our present behavior, both positive and negative, is the result of our personal history from embryo to puberty, or about the first 13 years of life. Your mother and father, not horrible demons inside you, are the source of your emotional problems.

Some people have difficulty in recalling their childhood, as if the forgetfulness were so strong that it is irreversible. Nonsense. Anything that influenced us must have been in the awareness at some level and can be brought back to the awareness with the proper tools. You are not a prisoner of your unconscious. Everything you need to know to understand how and why you became the way you are is available for recall and re-examination if you learn how to do it. Fortunately, once in the awareness, negative love patterns can be dealt with and eliminated no matter how deeply they may have been buried. (How this is done is discussed in some detail in the second half of this book.)

At this point many books say, or imply, something like: "Now that you know why you're doing all those awful things to yourself, STOP. Now go and sin no more." With negative love it's not that simple. If your jaw hurts, and you say to yourself, "I need to have my tooth filled," that won't be enough to solve your problem. You must then go and have the problem corrected.

In the same way, you cannot just decide to be different than you have been conditioned to be. Breaking free of the negative love trap requires work on the emotional, intellectual, and spiritual levels. Since the intellect is like a speck on an ocean of emotion, simply reading about emotional negative love patterns only enables you to learn more about how you "ought" to be with yourself and others, without removing the negative love pattern itself. The result is only more conflict between intellectually based knowledge and the emotional resistance to change.

At the same time that a part of you is "trying" to get free, another part is fighting change with all the guile, strength, and resourcefulness it can muster. We have already seen it as the negative emotional child, which is the part of you that never got past age 13 and is still negatively in love with Mommy and

Daddy. While your intellect and body may have continued to grow, your emotional self still behaves as a child.

It is the negative emotional child that resists change and growth. Thus, people often go into therapies of one kind or another telling themselves they sincerely want to stop suffering and solve their problems. In fact, it is often their intellect that knows they would be happier if they solved their problems, while the child inside is content to remain negatively in love with the parents. For at some point there comes a critical choice: being "true" to Mommy and Daddy or breaking free and risking the loss of their love. It is as if the person, secretly but fully comprehending what is really involved in change, says to himself, "If that's what it takes to get well, I think I'll stay sick. For a while longer, anyway."

Often people are not ready to put their lives together until they are down so low they have to reach up to touch bottom. Then they are usually ready to take responsibility for themselves and do something to change. Responsibility alone is not the full truth, for we did not make ourselves neurotic. We learned to be neurotic at our parents' misguidance and example. Therefore, to upbraid ourselves or others with being responsible for our problems is simply another admonition leading to further conflict and grief. Self-blame only adds to the misery while doing nothing to promote change or relief.

On the other hand, if you know what the problem is, and you have the tools and power to solve it, it does make good sense to free yourself. As you will see further on, life is beautiful without negative love. If you learned how to make yourself miserable, with the right help you can learn to make yourself happy.

Change *is* possible. After all, the key word in the definition of negative love is *adopt.* When expressing negative love, the traits are yours only by adoption. In truth they are not yours; they are not inherently *you.* They are not hereditary or genetically based. There is nothing inevitable or fated in what you became in response to the emotional blackmail by your parents. The growth of the emotional cancer, no matter how long it's been going on or how severe its consequences, is reversible. You learned how to be neurotic, and you can learn how to be free.

Do people really change through identifying and learning

how to drop their negative love patterns? Here is a note from a young woman named Mary Ellen. At age 33 she had recently left the cloistered life of a nun. Although physically beautiful, she was frightened, lonely, brow knitted, unhappy, irritable, frustrated, and paranoid. She was almost literally frightened of her own shadow.

> I bought a secondhand wooden table, Bob, which proved to be a perfect physical, tangible expression of what we're doing on a psychological level. The table was such a mess on top. At first glance, it seemed almost unsalvageable. There were circles of ink penetrating the wood, burnt marks where hot objects had been unthinkingly placed, and deep cuts where people had ignorantly and carelessly used knives. The more I sanded, the more sympathy I began to have for this poor, defenseless piece of wood. It was so marred by carelessness and ignorance. When I got through the layers of dirt and the old finish, I could begin to see a really beautiful wood grain underneath. Interestingly enough, as I sanded it, I began to identify with the table. I was having a very bad time previously putting blame for my scarred, ugly, deficient self on everybody except me. It was true, I was not good enough. I simply deserved to be abandoned, like the table was by its previous owner. But as I sanded, I began to feel, by the very physical act of removing the scars, this poor, defenseless table really mirrored me as I had been in the past. And as the scars were removed—true, with great *effort and difficulty*—I am sure that the table could feel, with great pain, *my* scars. I knew then that all the bad trips laid on me could also be removed. I now understand this. The table, now beautiful, with a brand-new finish, stands in my living room.

What Mary Ellen and others like her discovered through that beautiful experience with the table is that the world as she had known it was a lie. By removing the scars of the table, she was able to return it to the beauty of what it was. By removing the emotional cancer of lovelessness caused by the "virus" of negative love, she was able to return to the beauty she was before she adopted her parents' negativities. In the Process she was able to stop the war between her intellect and her emotions. In place of that conflict she was able to resume being her Quadrinity, which is the term I use for the fully integrated four aspects of each person: intellect, emotions, spirit, and physical body. Once negative love is dropped by the emotional child, the positive emotional child can mature and be integrated in whole, loving union with the present-day intellect, spirit, and body. That is the precious gift available to everyone once they get a loving divorce from Mother and Dad and learn to love themselves.

3. "*Now* Will You Love Me?"

A book about love is incomplete without a discussion of its most powerful means of expression: sex. Often when I ask people, "How's you love life?" they think I mean, "How's your sex life?" Although closely related, the two are different.

Which brings us to another rude question. How *is* your sex life? Do you have the kind of sex you want as often as you want? Is sex a regular part of your life or something you only wish for? Is it varied enough to remain fresh and exciting for you? Or have you fallen into a familiar pattern that is comfortable but dull? Does the fulfillment meet your anticipation? Or are you usually left feeling empty and blue after sex?

Beside your own pleasure, do you give sexual pleasure to your partner? Are you happy pleasing the other person? Do you give to give, or only give to get something in return? While thinking of your answers, remember that in sex, as in love, it takes courage and honesty to face the truth.

How do you relate to your sex partner? Is it someone you value and care deeply about? Someone who values you and cares deeply for you? Or are you virtual strangers, using each other's bodies for a brief attempt to escape from boredom or loneliness?

Is your sexual relationship solely that, or do you also share other parts of your life with your partner? Is your sex partner part of your life before and after sex? Are you able to share tender, intimate moments together afterward as well as before and during sex? (If you have more than one sexual partner, answer the questions for each one.)

More importantly, how do you feel about your sexuality? How do you compare with your ideal for a person of your sex, age, and background? If you aren't expressing your sexuality the way you think a man or woman should, how far short are you falling?

You can get the most benefit from this book by taking a few moments to think about your answers to these questions. Many people find it helpful to make notes of their self-observations in order not to lose the clarity of their first thoughts. It's sometimes difficult, painful, or discouraging to see how we are really living our sex lives. It's worth it, though, because looking is the only way to confront the problems and learn what to do about them.

What about your parents? Look at their sex life in the same way. Did they have the kind of sexual life they wanted? Were they able to give pleasure to each other with a mixture of passion and tenderness, variety and humor? Was sex a regular, joyous part of their lives, or an obligation they reluctantly fulfilled out of duty to each other?

How did they feel about their own sexuality? Was your father secure in his masculinity, or did he constantly have to prove himself with conquests and affairs? Did he seek sexual fulfillment away from home? Was your mother secure in her femininity, or did she need constant reassurance that she was an attractive, sexual woman? Did she also have to look elsewhere for the sexual pleasure a wife wants with her husband?

Some people may resist the suggestion that they look at their parents' sex life since they never actually saw their parents "doing it," or they feel they are prying into private matters. Actually having seen them in bed together isn't necessary in order to understand their sex life together. Did they display love, affection, and warmth for each other? And for you? If they never touched you, it's likely they seldom touched each other. Were they able to joke about sex from time to time? Or was sex so filled with taboos and prohibitions that they wouldn't allow themselves to laugh at it?

Look also at how they handled your sexual education. How did your parents teach you the facts of life? As you approached adolescence, did they talk about it comfortably with you? Were they able to give you clear, reliable information about the changes in your body as you became a physical adult? Were they able to deal compassionately and reassuringly with your questions and fears? Were they also able to share with you the joy of your joining them in adulthood? Were they able to give you the emotional maturity needed to prepare you for real adult sexuality? If you had a sexual problem right now, could you discuss it frankly with your mother and father?

Or did they avoid the subject and duck their responsibility to you? Did they perhaps slip you a book and say, "Here, read this"? Did they leave it to some other adult, perhaps a doctor, schoolteacher, or religious counselor to assist you through this critical transition in your life?

Or did they do nothing at all, leaving you to fend for yourself, almost certain to pick up misinformation and superstitions from your equally uninformed friends?

Have you had difficulty rising above your parents' level of sexual knowledge? Could you easily and knowingly tell a 12-year-old boy or girl the facts of sexual life without sniggering as if sex were dirty or stammering as if sex were frightening? Can you accurately describe the structure and function of the sexual and reproductive organs in man and woman? Could you tell a naïve youngster what he or she needs to know about masturbation, birth control, and venereal disease? Could you tell a young man or woman how to enjoy sex without exploiting others? And can you back up your instruction with your own living example? Would you advise a young person to live his or her sexual life as you have lived yours? And would they be wise to follow your counsel? Or would you have to cop out and say, "Do as I say, not as I do"?

Sure, these are tough questions. Almost no one who answers honestly will be completely satisfied with what he sees in himself. The 98 percent of the world who have love problems also have sexual problems. My point is that discomfort with sex proves parents had sexual difficulties that continue as a negative influence today. If your mother and father did not have an adequate sexual adjustment coupled with feelings of love and tenderness for each other, they couldn't teach these qualities to you. Children of sexually confused, frightened, ignorant, defensive, or prudish parents are presented with two unsatisfactory choices. They can adopt mother's and father's basically unhealthy, immature sexual attitudes along with their awkwardness or ignorance about sex. Or they can rebel against mother's and father's example, attempting to be free of their influence while covering up the conflict that inevitably follows on the heels of rebellion. Either way, the result is a stunted, incomplete sex life.

Nor are the children of "liberated" parents much better off. Where sex is treated as casually as if it were just another physical function like eating or moving your bowels, children are cheated of the opportunity to see the spiritual and emotional side of sexual love. Don't assume that if mother and father had no sexual inhibitions that they therefore had no sexual problems. The inability to see beyond the physical side of sex to its emotional, spiritual, and intellectual dimensions is as much a problem as the common inability to fully enjoy the physical experience of it.

After looking at mother's and father's sex life, compare it with your own. If you are living your sexual life differently than your parents did, either more permissively or more conservatively, is it easy for you? Are you really free of the example they set for you? Or do you have to struggle against pangs of guilt or anger for rebelling against them?

On the other hand, if your sex life is similar to theirs, how do you like it? Would you change it if you could? How much would things have to change for you to be happy, however you define happiness?

Like the ability to love, the ability to enjoy adult sexuality without guilt or fear does not depend on conditions "out there," such as your partner's ability to turn you on. Sexual pleasure comes from your freedom to turn yourself on. We learn, or more often don't learn, to enjoy a full sexual life by the example our parents set for us. Does this mean parents should invite their teen-age children into the bedroom with them? Of course not. Parents have a right to their privacy. Being sexually honest with children doesn't necessarily mean discussing your own sexual problems with them, either. But to give them adequate preparation for adult life, parents must acknowledge the existence of sexual life to their children.

If you are among the 2 per cent who know how to love, you know what I am talking about. The sexual experience goes beyond passion to include tenderness, variety, humor, openness, strength, and surrender. While sexual fulfillment is affected by whom you are with and what you are doing, the level you reach is ultimately up to you. If you are not bound to mother and father by the strings of negative love, you are open to positive sex as a total experience. The body becomes alive, aware and open to total sensuality. Complete sex encompasses your entire self: the spiritual essence, the emotional goodness, and yes, the intellectual ability to understand what's happening. All four parts of you, body, spirit, emotions, and intellect, merge with the deepest levels of the other in a blending that expresses complete, momentary union.

Most of us never reach the heights of sexual ecstasy on all four levels of being because the fetters of negative love bind us. Sexuality is controlled by negative love like any other area of life. Whether parents are aware of it or not, they determine how their child expresses sex. Whether a child becomes masculine or feminine, tough or tender, lusty or frustrated, hot or cold, promiscuous or celibate, is determined by the negative love programming inflicted on him during his childhood and the manner in which he expresses the programming during adulthood.

Sexual difficulties, however distressing they may be, are only symptoms of a deeper problem: the inability to love. It is necessary to work through the symptom to the cause. The remedy for sexual problems is the same as for all neurotic problems: love that nourishes the individual and enables him to share that emotional goodness with others. Love for self and others leads you easily and effortlessly toward that which promotes your growth and fulfillment, in sex as in every other aspect of life.

For a deeper understanding of sex, let's look beneath the apparent diversity of sexual behavior to an important unity: the emotion behind the act. Instead of asking, "What are people doing sexually?" let's ask, "Why are people doing this, and how do they feel about it?" Love, hate, jealousy, anger, fear, pity, contempt, sadness, are the same for each of us regardless of how we express them.

What we do comes out of how we feel. Our sexual behavior comes out of our negative love relations with our parents during childhood. By asking "Why?" instead of "What?" we get not hundreds, or perhaps thousands, of categories of behavior but only the two aspects of the negative love pattern: negative love or rebellion. When a child adopts the traits, moods, and admonitions of his parents, he is expressing negative love for them. In rebellion, the child rejects mother and father and chooses from among the variety of contrary ways to engage in sex. As in all other areas of life, sexual rebellion leads to conflict because the programmed child within the adult is risking the loss of Mommy's and Daddy's love by disobeying them. ("Child within the adult" refers to the emotional part of us that is stuck in the past, still relating to the mother and father we knew during childhood. Unfinished emotional business does not go away by itself.) When parents send mixed messages or set an inconsistent example, children become confused and frightened. As a result, most people show a mixture of negative love and rebellion.

One of the more common sexual problems is boredom. Sometimes sex becomes more a duty than a pleasure. Women are "supposed" to do it, so the woman does it. But she takes no real joy in it. Housewives with children at home often have this problem, although it isn't limited to them. Women who work, both married and single, are also prone to suffer from the sexual blahs. Men, of course, experience this, too.

The sexual wasteland is created by parents who didn't enjoy sex and couldn't teach their children to enjoy it. Often mother was a drudge who worked so hard she had no time or energy left for any joyful sex with her husband, and the tone in her house was drab and tense from fatigue and overwork. Father was usually aloof and undemonstrative, showing little affection for his wife or his children.

Sexually bored women are usually relating to mother and father with simple negative love. Mother was overworked, overfed, underpaid, and underloved, and daughter is living her own life the same way. "See, Mom and Dad?" her negative emotional child is saying. "Life's a drag just like you said. No time for fun, especially sex. I'm just like you. *Now* will you love me?"

Men, too, get similar programming: "Sex is no fun. Work hard and forget about it." In fact, people with this programming tend to marry each other and live out their boring lives together. Like his wife, the husband in such a marriage expresses his negative love to his parents by marrying someone who is hard-working and unsexual. His mother, like his wife, was so overworked and underappreciated that she had little time or energy to show any love or enthusiasm for her husband. Out of negative love to mother, he married a girl "just like the girl who married dear old Dad."

He also expresses his negative love for father by becoming like him. From him he got the admonition, "Wives aren't sexual. Settle down and forget sex." Which is what he does. His father, like his wife's father, was unimaginative, distant, undemonstrative, and usually not fully *there* for his wife and children. Through their negative love programming the two were made for each other.

Both the husband and the wife in this situation would prefer to rebel and live the fuller lives they were truly made for, but they are so trapped in negative love that they cannot live differently without plunging themselves into deep conflict and guilt. Most of the time their lives are not unbearable since their hard work often gives them money enough for more than necessities. They tend not to rock the boat or cause trouble, but below the surface they lead "lives of quiet desperation."

The real problem for each of these people is not that they aren't getting enough sex. They certainly would feel better and have more fun if they were getting more sex, but *their real problem is no love.* Mother and father taught them to be polite and well-behaved, which is to say, phony. Their relationship with each other is flat and mechanical because they go through the motions of family life while not experiencing the warmth of love that make the family more than a physical convenience or an economic advantage. Born out of love for each other, sex is no chore but an excitement to share. Instead of dragging at the end of the day, he's eager to get home to her, and she's eager to have him come home to her. They love to be together, for each is the best friend to the other. When the tone is loving, each loves to be there and loves to take the other to bed (or wherever they love to have sex) and make sure the other isn't bored or unhappy.

Boredom isn't the only way to adopt the negative love traits of mother and father. The wildest kind of compulsive, promiscuous sexing can also be an expression of negative love. "Like father, like son" applies to sex as to other areas. Often the man who chases every woman in sight, married or single, young or old, is imitating what he saw his father doing (or what his father wished *he* had done in his own youth). If his mother also had casual sexual affairs, a man's pattern of much sex with no emotional involvement will be a double negative love adoption of their traits. His father's admonition may have been, "Women are there for the taking, but don't get trapped." And mother's silent or overt admonition is often complementary, "Women are for sex but not love."

"See, Mom and Dad?" says his negative emotional child within, "I'm having lots of sex just the way you did. But I'm not letting anyone fulfill me any more than you did, so I'm not outdoing you. I'm still your little boy. *Now* will you love me?"

To avoid outdoing mother and father, the compulsive sexer, male or female, will usually run from anyone who appears to offer real emotional involvement or asks for real emotional commitment. In adopting negative love traits, the slogan, no matter what the behavior, reflects the idea from one of the old gospel songs: "It was good for my mother; it was good for my father; and it's good enough for me."

People with compulsive sexual appetites rarely get more than a temporary and superficial pleasure from sex because there is no warm feeling behind it for them. When sex is only physical, there is always something missing. Men and women with no experience of the nonphysical dimensions of sex may know that something is missing without being able to describe it adequately. Often they search for many years for the ultimate sexual experience that will make it happen. It never does because what they seek is not only physical but emotional and spiritual, the very levels of being their parents didn't develop in them during childhood. Out of negative love to mother and father they remain one-dimensional beings.

Adopting an admonition from mother or father doesn't necessarily mean becoming like them, as the following story shows. Charles was a fragile, effeminate boy, a great disappointment to his masculine, heterosexual father. His father tried without success to coax, cajole, or threaten his son into behaving like a typical rough-and-tumble boy. Instead, Charles was an indoor type who made good grades in school, which only heightened his father's frustration since he himself had been a poor student.

Although Charles rebelled against his father's masculine traits, he adopted a deeper, more powerful admonition from his father: "You are a pansy. Get away from me." In reply his negative emotional child said: "OK, Dad, whatever you say. I am a pansy. *Now* will you love me?" Charles never lost his deep longing for his father's love, so he sought it in this illogical way. Each person's negative love syndrome is a mixture of adoption and rebellion. Charles showed both, but his dominant theme was adopting the admonition, which caused his homosexuality to manifest itself.

When he was old enough to leave home, he moved to a large city, fell in with a group of homosexuals, and lived like the "pansy" his father said he was. As a soft type, he was attractive to masculine men who resembled his father. Charles sought from them the male approval and acceptance he desperately wanted and had missed as a child.

He also expressed negative love for his mother through his homosexuality. She felt guilty for producing a "queer" son and for not really wanting him. To cover her guilt, she overreacted, smothering him with attention and protection, especially when her husband would berate the boy for his lack of toughness and masculinity. After each brutal tongue-lashing, Charles would run to her and bury his face in her bosom while she stroked his hair and soothed his crushed self-respect. "There, there," she would purr. "It's all right. Mother understands. Sit here while I dress, and we'll go for a walk together." Boys learn to be masculine by growing away from their mothers and toward their fathers. Charles continued to stay close to his mother since she was the only source of warmth for him. While remaining close to his mother, he grew more and more distant from his father. His mother could do little to stop her husband from cruelly taunting the boy since she felt guilty and responsible for his feminine ways.

Obviously, not all male homosexuals had rejecting fathers and smothering, overprotective mothers. Homosexuality, like any other sexual orientation or preference, has a number of potential sources, far too many to cover completely here. Some men got along very well with father, but mother was so cold and distant that they adopted the admonition "Women are unloving" from both parents. In adulthood we create our own emotional world based on what we were taught to expect. For a boy with a warm father and cold mother, his adult world may contain warm men as friends and lovers but only cold, hateful women. Here, too, the negative emotional child is saying, "You were right, Mom and Dad. A man's best friend is another man."

Homosexuals, both male and female, are not sick, any more than are their heterosexual brothers and sisters. Most are caught up in negative love patterns that determine how their inherent sexuality is expressed, and most need to learn how to love themselves and others on all four levels of their being. With self-love, homosexuals can also have healthy, loving relationships.

Parents also teach their children to be afraid of sex. Often a frigid woman had a mother who taught her that sex was dirty and disgusting. Out of straight negative love to mother, the girl will adopt mother's trait. In adult life she may avoid sex completely by never having any male friends. Even if she marries, though, she will often avoid sex by choosing a male as unsexual as she is.

A woman's sexual fears may also come from her father, as in the following story. One morning as she was getting out of bed, little Alice heard her father whistling as he shaved in the bathroom. Tiptoeing behind him, she saw that he was naked. He was absorbed in his morning ritual and didn't hear the barefoot girl. Silently easing her head around his leg, she saw his penis hanging limp between his thighs. She had never seen one before.

"Daddy," she asked, pointing with delight at her discovery, "what's that?"

Startled and embarrassed, he replied angrily, "None of your business! You'll find out soon enough. Leave me alone."

"But, Daddy . . . ," she stammered, "I . . . I . . ."

"Never mind," he barked as he quickly reached for a towel to wrap around his waist. "Get out of here! And don't come in here again without knocking."

Crushed, Alice slunk away, vowing never again to be curious about that thing between Daddy's legs. As she grew older, she learned that it was a penis and that it had something to do with sex. But her powerful negative love admonition said, "Don't be curious about a man's penis, or he'll get angry and yell at you." To our adult intellect this may seem illogical or absurd, but to a 4-year-old—and to the negative emotional child within an adult like Alice—it makes good sense. Whether she can remember it or not, every woman who is afraid of sex with a man has in her childhood one or more scenes of traumatic fear similar to this. These unfortunate women dare not disobey those admonitions of fear without risking the loss of mother's and father's love they so desperately crave. No matter how much time passes, or even how patient and understanding their husbands or lovers might be, women whose fathers or mothers frightened them and disapproved of their sexual curiosity are doomed to live sexless lives until they are free to stop adopting the negative love admonitions they heard as little girls.

The impotent man, like the frigid woman, is the product of his parents' teaching. While what they tell him may not be clearly about sex, it can nonetheless have a powerful sexual impact. As a young boy, for example, the impotent man may have heard his father violently and repeatedly flail him with the taunt, "You're an idiot! You can't do anything right." Since disobeying his father means risking the loss of his love, the boy will often adopt the admonition that he can't do anything right, including sex. Later in life, when his chance with a willing woman arrives, his negative love for father may keep him from rising to the occasion.

Or his mother may have taught him to be afraid of rejection by being alternately warm and cold toward him. On a seesaw of love, he never learned whether he deserved love or not. He got just enough taste of a woman's love to want more, but he's afraid to go all the way, in love or in sex, for fear the woman will coldly reject him the way mother often did.

Since he fears that whatever he does won't be good enough, this type of man often chooses not to risk failure and rejection, and avoids sex after a few youthful attempts. The tragedy is that often these men have normal sexual appetites, but their fear of failure keeps them from taking the risks that are necessary to succeed at anything difficult and worth doing. That old crippling message from mother and father, "You're not good enough to please me," makes it impossible for the man to take his place among sexually mature individuals. Instead, he will remain his parents' incompetent little boy as long as he continues to reply, "OK, Mom and Dad. I'm the bungler you always said I was. *Now* will you love me?"

Sex therapy is of limited value in such cases. While frigid women and impotent men can be taught how to make intercourse possible, the level of sexual fulfillment is limited by the continuing effects of the negative love programming that says, in effect, "Sex is a no-no," and "You'll never make it." This problem of competing messages between our parents and the world around us is particularly painful in this day of sexual openness. We hear messages that say, "Go ahead! Break free. Do it, whatever turns you on." Breaking free can mean almost anything: having sex without marriage; using birth control; experimenting with oral sex; taking an extramarital lover; having an abortion; or experiencing interracial sex, homosexuality, and sex with strangers. I believe in freedom and have dedicated my life to helping others find it. But it's impossible to skip and jump through the fields of sexual bliss with the ball and chain of negative love around your ankle. Breaking free means disobeying the admonition, "Don't be freer than Mommy and Daddy or we won't love you." What sexually unfree men and women struggle against is not the social rules of the time in which they live but the spoken or implied confining sexual messages they received when they were children.

It is a mistake, therefore, for sex counselors and therapists to tell troubled men and women to learn to free themselves sexually. The real negative love programming is usually below the level of awareness, and people cannot be ordered, coaxed, or persuaded out of it. Attempting to do so merely causes more conflict and tension.

Linda came from a family in which love was just a word. Her mother was cold and aloof toward the occasional sexual advances of her father, who sought relief in work, sports, and an occasional "night on the town with the boys." With no physical touching from either parent, she grew up desperately longing for warmth of any kind. Although her parents didn't teach her to be sexual, she was a pretty girl, and boys were attracted to her. Soon after her fourteenth birthday she had her first sexual experience with a boy. Although at first awkward and fumbling, she quickly learned that boys, and later men, would give her the warmth and approval she never got at home. Her parents attempted to stop what they called "her decline into wantonness and sin," but once she had a taste of warmth and approval, she couldn't get enough. When she ran away at 17, her emotional child said, "The hell with you. I'm going where I can have some fun and get some love. I'll show you." And so she did, gaining a reputation wherever she went as a warm, sexually free woman. Below her sexually free exterior, though, she was in terrible conflict over her rebellion. The more she tried, and failed, to get Daddy's love from her many sex partners, the more frustrated and empty she felt. She couldn't give up sex because it felt good, and it was her ticket to popularity, but she couldn't really enjoy it on a deep level, either, because it went counter to mother's and father's admonition, "Don't be sexy. Don't touch people." Her tragedy, like that of many beautiful women who appear so loving, is that behind the façade lies desperate emptiness.

Almost any behavior contrary to the parents' sexual traits and admonitions will "work" as a form of rebellion because it is often indulged in not for its own sake but to get even with unloving mother and father. Women from families in which little love is shown, or in which the sexing is high and loose, may rebel in a socially acceptable way by withdrawing from the world of adult sex, perhaps by joining a religious order. Rebellion need not be unconventional or unpopular to be effective. It only needs to go counter to what mother and father said and did.

Rebellion stemming from sibling rivalry usually has its sexual aspects as well. When a little girl feels displaced by her younger sister, for example, she may decide that no more positive attention is available and settle for her parents' negative attention. In conventional middle-class families this often appears as the goody-goody younger sister who compliantly marries a professional man and moves to the suburbs to raise well-behaved children, while her displaced older sister angrily rebels by not marrying and instead goes through a series of brief, superficial affairs that leave her feeling empty and exploited but "free of their bourgeois morality."

When she does marry, the middle-class rebel often chooses the type of man her parents have the least regard for: an artist or other creative type who feeds her beans and hope. Often she may work to support him, which serves to further outrage her parents' rigid sense of propriety. While she genuinely suffers from the physical and financial deprivations of the artistic life, her inner emotional child gleefully watches her parents' distress. "I showed *those* assholes. They wouldn't love me, so I ran away, and now they're sorry, aren't they? Look at me. Aren't I free?" Their tragedy is that their intellect knows they might be happier doing things differently from their parents, yet their emotions deny them the pleasure of real freedom.

The negative love pattern is the same with brothers as with sisters. If one brother, either younger or older, gets all the positive attention, the other will often rebel, deciding that opposing mother and father is the way to get their negative attention. The bizarre, often destructive sexual lives of many single persons, either divorced or never married, are proof not of their freedom but of their angry childhood desire to rebel against mother and father. "See, Mommy and Daddy. Since you won't love me, I won't do what you want me to do. I'll get into trouble, and you'll be sorry. *Then* maybe you'll notice me."

Sexual rebellion can also be delayed until the middle years or later. The escapades of men and women in their forties and fifties are often the result of the years they compliantly bought mother's and father's pseudo-love by being "good," while receiving no genuine love in return. As the middle of life approaches, and their parents begin to die off, many say to themselves, "The hell with it. I'm going to have some fun while there is still time." Such rebellions are usually brief, because they bring painful conflict with them, and rebellion never leads to love.

The reality of sexual life is sometimes even more complicated. Often a child receives mixed or contradictory sexual messages from his parents. When mother and father don't agree on sex, their children are left confused, frightened, and bitter as they flip-flop between pleasing father and pleasing mother.

Michael's story is typical of the child with inconsistent parents. His father, a tough, masculine type, taught him that sex was OK but that only sissies showed their feelings. His mother, a meek, clinging woman, was frightened of sex and never discussed it but showed him it was OK to feel hurt or frightened. Michael's deep sexual conflict was inevitable. With a father who said, "Do it like a man," and a mother who said, "Sex is dirty," he was wrong no matter what he did. Obeying father, he compulsively chased women he had no feelings for while his negative emotional child asked, "How am I doing, Dad?" He had sex out of negative love to father but felt guilty over his rebellion against mother. At other times he obeyed mother and went long periods without sex while feeling depressed and lonely, which was rebellion against father. Back and forth he went, feeling guilty for mother when he was having sex and unmanly for father when he wasn't. Michael was ripped apart by this conflict until he learned how to free himself from his negative love patterns.

Ruth's parents were more closely attuned in their sexual messages to their daughter, but she nonetheless found herself in a double-bind conflict. Her father thought casual sex was OK for men, telling her older brother, "Find 'em, feel 'em, fuck'em, forget 'em." Since children often adopt messages meant for a sibling, she adopted this one as her own. Her mother thought sex was OK, but not before marriage. "Nice girls don't do it except with their husbands" was the way Ruth's mother put it.

As she grew to adulthood, Ruth felt bad no matter what she did. She didn't stop wanting the casual sex father advocated merely because mother told her to wait until the wedding. And she didn't stop hearing mother's forbidding voice in her head even after she decided to have sex with the next man who found her. When Mommy says, "No!" and Daddy says, "Go!" the emotional result can be pure hell.

The man or woman who lives two sexual lives, one public, the other private, also responds to his conventional parents with both negative love and rebellion. A closet homosexual with a wife and children lives in this split pattern. Out of negative love he leads a conventional, straight life most of the time. When he rebels occasionally, he finds a male partner and lives out his sexual fantasies. At the height of his orgasm with another man his negative emotional child may be riding high: "Whoopee! Fun, fun, fun." Later, he may be thrown into guilt and remorse: "Gee, I'm sorry, Daddy. I couldn't help myself. If I feel bad enough about it, will you forgive me and love me?" His intellect may not hear the conversation, but his emotions sense the roar of conflict.

Negative love patterns are even more obvious in the extremes of sexuality, such as violence or total deprivation. If Daddy was a sadist who beat up mother before having sex with her, the child learns that screams and bruises are the proper kind of sexual foreplay. Many sadists and masochists cannot be sexually aroused in any other way, completely because of their negative love programming. When they are relieved of their unfortunate emotional attachment to their destructive parents, they can respond sexually as if they had never heard of the Marquis de Sade.

Women of sadistic tendencies are not necessarily imitating mother. Daddy is more often the culprit here. If he was cold or rarely home, she may be getting even with him by mistreating her masochistic husband or boyfriend. (The daughters of cold men get even more places than in bed, in case you haven't been in divorce court or a shopping center lately.)

The nymphomaniac, too, suffers from a severe lack of father's love, often through death or abandonment. So deprived was she that no man can satisfy her, in bed or out, though she searches desperately from one bed to another for one who will. Even while she runs to a new sex alliance, her emotional child is saying, "It's OK, Daddy. I won't let anyone fulfill me if I can't have you. I'll always be yours no matter who tries to take your place."

The rapist is dying of thirst for mother's love. When he cried in the night as an infant, mother ignored him or turned the music up. He could only get her attention by crying still louder. As he grew older he became even more demanding. He had to *take* what she wouldn't freely give him. When he rapes a resisting, terrified woman he's in effect still taking from his unloving, resisting mother and getting even with her for the heartless, rejecting way she treated him as a child. His guilt and conflict stem from the pain of his negative emotional child, who gets "love" in this way.

There are many variations in the kinds of negative love programming leading to sexual deviance. We cannot cover them all here, but sex deviants in general are people who were pathetically deprived of love during childhood. The child molester, the voyeur, the fetishist, were all so absolutely love starved and unfulfilled that they strive for what appear to be odd or disgusting sexual outlets. The child molester is often reliving the relationship with a younger sister or brother. Depending on whether he's violent or harmless, he's either getting even with the rival who displaced him, or trying to prove that he really loved the rival whom he may have bullied and abused the first time around. In some cases the child molester watched as his mother gave her love to a neighbor's child while ignoring him. In turning his adult sexual attention toward a child, he is acting out of negative love and rebellion. He adopts mother's trait by appearing to love the little girl or little boy. ("See, Mother, I'm loving a small child just the way you did. *Now* will you love me?") At the same time, his abuse of the child is a way of getting even with mother for not giving him the love he so desperately wanted. And still wants.

The fetishist may have an amazing variety of peculiar sexual turn-ons. Whether his lust is for feet, underwear, shoes, vegetables, or the living room furniture, he takes the thing as a substitute for his childhood love: mother. Anything strongly linked with her in his mind will act as a trigger for his childhood longing. The voyeur, or Peeping Tom, suffers from an unsatisfied sexual curiosity. If mother made too big a fuss when he caught an accidental look at her while she was undressed, he may develop an overpowering desire to find out what the great secret is.

The spectrum of negative love and sex is much wider than one chapter can encompass. These few examples show how some common sexual problems grow out of the programming parents inflict on their children. No matter what the sexual problem, the answer is the same—love, enough to fill the void left by the parents who, for whatever reason, were not there in the way they were needed most: cherishing and accepting, breathing into us not only life's fire but love's warmth.

4. Mind Revelations

If negative love to mother and father is *the* problem facing us, what is the solution? What can anyone do about it?

The answer is, was, and always will be the same: "the flowing, the rendering, the outgoing of the heart and soul of emotional goodness, to yourself first, then to those around you." The antidote to the poison of negative love is the power of *positive* love, first directed inward to yourself, then sent forth to those around you.

The real question is . . . How? How can you teach someone to love; to overcome years, perhaps an entire lifetime, of negative feelings and behavior? How can a man or woman rise above the muck and mire of negative love to the heights of positive love?

The way out is the same as the way in: programming. The negative love syndrome is a destructive form of mind programming. Mother's and father's negative traits, and the rebellion against them, are adopted, not genetic. Not loving yourself and others is like any bad habit. You can learn to love by demolishing the negative love programming and replacing it with positive programming that frees you to be your true self.

The Fischer-Hoffman Process* teaches love in exactly this

*See the Appendix following Chapter 12 for the story of the origin and development of the Fischer-Hoffman Process.

way, by showing people how the negative patterns that plague and distress them arise from the negative love programs they received from their parents during childhood. Greater awareness alone, however, is not enough. The Process also provides the tools to break up the programming that keeps you from being both spontaneous and autonomous.

To many people this description of how to teach love may seem too pat, too simple. Yet the most powerful truths are often the most simple. To love or not to love is a matter of one's childhood training. Since it is a matter of training, love can be learned through a process of retraining.

The Fischer-Hoffman Process is based on the premise that each of us is a four-part being, or Quadrinity. The physical aspect is the body. It includes the brain, which is the organic structure that makes mental activity possible. The nonphysical aspect has three parts: (1) the spirit, (2) the intellect, and (3) the emotions. Taken together, these three comprise the nonphysical Mind Trinity.

While we believe the spiritual self is a crucial aspect of each person, learning self-love does not depend on one's belief in spirituality or God. As one student said, "I didn't believe in the psychic stuff before I took the Process, and I don't believe in it now. But the Process still worked for me."

The negative love programming is recorded chiefly in our emotions during childhood. It also affects our intellect and obscures our perfect spiritual self. The push and pull of conflict we experience stems from the lack of integration between the present-day intellect and childhood emotions. The specific goal of reprogramming is to re-educate the emotional child within to drop its negative programming, grow up, and join its spiritual self and intellectual self in present-day harmony. When this newly mature Trinity merges with the physical self and becomes a total Quadrinity, the individual is free to act, think, feel, and most of all, to love as one with no conflict or inhibition. After being relieved of the negative love programming that keeps you fragmented, there is no more question of which part of you is running your life. There's just you, acting, feeling, thinking, and *being* love. Lack of integration in the Quadrinity is so common that most people mistakenly assume the split is natural. It is not. The integrated Quadrinity of body, spirit, intellect, and emotions is the way we were meant to be.

The programming from childhood, both positive and negative, is recorded in our minds much like information is recorded on a computer card. When the "computer card mind" is "inserted" into the physical brain, we behave according to the programming. Our brain does what our mind orders it to do. To experience how your mind programs your brain, close your eyes and see yourself in a supermarket. . . . (As you read, pause at the dots to visualize the scene fully.) Walk over to the fresh produce section. . . . Note a large bin of beautiful, thick-skinned navel oranges. They have a heavy orange aroma. Select one. Mentally hold it in your hands and feel the pores of the skin . . . Smell it . . . Dig your fingers into the orange skin and peel it . . . Segment it and plop a juicy morsel into your mouth . . . Feel the orange juices flow across your gums and down your throat . . . Taste the sweetness . . . Now mentally walk to a counter of lemons and select a large, yellow lemon . . . Smell its lemony aroma . . . Nearby there's a knife and cutting board. Place the lemon on the cutting board and slice it in two . . . Put half the lemon in your mouth and suck on it . . . Do you feel your mouth pucker? Are you salivating?

What you just experienced is an example of a mind revelation, a psychological procedure that exposes hidden truths of your mind, often with dramatic effect. Mind revelations are not occult or mysterious. They are the ordinary reality of life. They are the key to finding and experiencing your own positive reality, not by intellectual insights but with deep emotional force. Your physical reaction to the orange and lemon mind revelation demonstrates how the mind can be used to cause physiological activity. Although you didn't eat any fruit, *your body responded to the directions of your brain as if you had.* Similarly, although with more complexity and sophistication, mind revelations can be used to reprogram the negative patterns to positive ones.

While doing this mind revelation, you probably saw some kind of mental picture. There are two kinds of mental pictures, similar in appearance but different in origin. With the active imagination, which is under our control, we use our conscious minds intentionally to create an image.

Receptive visualizing, on the other hand, is what we allow

to enter our mind. Receptive visualizing often occurs while we are daydreaming or "staring off into space." Dreams are another kind of receptive, as opposed to active, seeing. The images are simply there, without our consciously summoning or directing them.

The ability to see mental images originating outside ourselves is part of everyone's natural sensory perception (NSP). Although many people are unaware of this part of their mental capacities, the ability is within each of us, waiting to be developed. Everyone can learn to see with the inner eye (in psychic terms known as clairvoyance) and hear with the inner ear (clairaudience). As with any other natural ability, some people have more potential than others, but everyone can see and hear psychically after some basic instruction and a brief period of practice.

One importance of NSP for the Process is that it gives clients a greater range of tools for reprogramming, beyond their everyday mental activities and memory. The mind is, of course, more than just the intellect. It has an important spiritual faculty that the Process helps develop—both for its own sake and as a tool for reprogramming.

Mind revelations are *receptive* visualizations, not projections. The following excerpt is taken from the Process notes of a man who discovered this for himself.

> You assigned us a mind revelation in class. We were to see ourselves in our bedroom and visualize the closest person to us entering who would call us by name and say something pleasant to us. In doing it, I tried to see my wife, but no go. I tried to see several others. Then all of a sudden my 13-year-old daughter appeared and said, "Daddy, I love you." I was surprised to find that my intended imagined projection of my wife didn't work in this mind realm. Instead of my wife, my daughter entered. Surprise! I now see that the mind revelations are not projected imagery.

With this brief preparation you are now ready to go on a mind revelation adventure. You will experience a place of peace, your personal sanctuary, and meet your spiritual guide and teacher. Have someone read the following to you or put it on tape and play it for yourself.

To help you relax, sit well back in your chair, gently close your eyes, take a deep breath with the soft sound of "i" as in "in," and exhale through your mouth with a long sound of *sch* (like letting air out of a balloon). I. . . . Sch. . . . Do this three times. When you feel yourself relaxed, you are ready.

Send your nonphysical self (your Trinity) out into space where there is total nothingness. See absolutely nothing . . . In front of you appears a large, rectangular white screen . . . The screen begins to descend slowly until it is out of the "picture" entirely. As it descends, you see a blue sky above the top of the screen . . . As the screen continues to descend, you see a tranquil refuge, a place that gives you a strong feeling of comfort and peace, perhaps a woodland meadow, a beach, or a mountain setting. See the trees, flowers, grass, and other details of this lovely natural setting. This is your sanctuary, in which you can recharge your energy and find tranquility, safety, and freedom.

In your mind's eye see yourself in the sanctuary. Take a leisurely walk along the pathways. Experience the beautiful feeling of belonging and unity. Feel the warmth of the sun caressing you. Listen to the song of the birds. You have found your mind's home.

As you walk along a path, you see in the distance a luminous white glow. It appears to be a circular light. You stop about five feet in front of it. As it slowly descends, you sense someone standing behind the light. First you see the hair. Note the color and style. Then, as the light continues to descend, see the shape of the forehead. Then a pair of beautiful, loving eyes appear. The disc descends further and there are cheekbones and a nose. Then the lips and the chin. The entire loving face is now visible. Note the sex of your guide.

Next the neck, shoulders, and torso appear. Note the mode of dress. Now all the features of your spiritual guide are revealed. Walk up to your guide without fear, reach for the face, and pull gently as if removing a mask. A true guide will not object. If the face comes off, you have encountered an impostor. Mentally tell the impostor to leave your sanctuary, continue walking along the path, and repeat the descending disc process as many times as necessary until you get a guide who cannot be unmasked.

When you have your real guide, ask his or her name. The

first thought impression you have is your guide's name. Accept what you hear or see.

Raise your hands, touch your fingertips to your guide's, and send energy to him or her. Speak to your guide mentally, saying, "Carve out thousands of acres of this lovely parkland as our private sanctuary. Please build a stone wall around it so high and so thick that no one can enter." He or she does so. You are now in a protected fortress sanctuary with your guide. Ask your guide to take you to the wall and blast a tunnel through it. Now have him or her erect solid bronze doors every 10 feet down the length of the tunnel. You hold the master key to these doors. You hand the key to your guide, saying, "As my spiritual guide and guardian, I trust you to protect me from all negative forces." Your guide then opens all the doors with the master key. Ask your guide to cleanse your sanctuary of all forces, both positive and negative, so that the sanctuary will be totally yours. He or she searches everywhere in the sanctuary and ushers out all psychic forces. The positive ones leave willingly, knowing there are other places for them. The negative forces don't want to leave, and your guide uses his or her power, coupled with yours, forcibly to eject all the negative forces from your sanctuary. They cannot withstand your combined strength and are drawn from the rivers, streams, lakes, beaches, and fields toward the doors. They fly past you and down the tunnel as if drawn by a giant vacuum machine attached to the outermost door of your sanctuary wall. Your guide then makes a last check of the sanctuary to be sure they are all out. He or she finds a last holdout behind a boulder. This most negative of all forces grips tenaciously to the boulder, but your guide's hypnotic gaze pries it loose and sends it plummeting down the tunnel.

As you and your guide stand at the tunnel door, he or she gently turns to you and asks you to disrobe. As you remove your clothing your guide peels off old encrusted negativities from your psychic body. This is the negative crud that has blighted you from the psychic side of life. As your guide removes the negativity from you, he or she tosses the pieces down the tunnel one by one. Your guide also looks deep within you, as if you were transparent, removes from you any lingering negative forms buried within you, sends them out the tunnel, and locks the door. Your guide holds his or her hands over your center and sends forth a warm light as a soothing balm to relieve any lingering pain. Feel a warm glow deep within yourself.

Your guide then takes you to a lovely watering place. The water is inviting. Plunge in. Delight yourself with the refreshing sensation of the water. Together you and your guide romp and splash like children. After playing, you ease onto your back and float. Lazily you let yourself drift with your guide. Later, as you bob against the edge of the water pool, you open your eyes, refreshed, and lift yourself onto the shore. Your guide gently towels you dry and gives you a garment similar to his or her own. You feel wonderful as you and your guide walk to a shaded glen and seat yourselves beneath a tree. Fragrant flowers abound.

As you sit side by side, you and your guide talk together as old, trusted friends. Ask your guide a question. He or she will answer. Take paper and pencil in hand and record the rest of your conversation. You have found your guide and sanctuary and may return to this place as often as you like, especially when you need a moment's peace and relaxation. Each time you do this your guide will give you the love and guidance you need to continue your journey.

If you have encountered anything frightening or negative so far, it is vital to use the mind revelation that follows. Again close your eyes, do three long *isch*es, relax and send your Trinity into empty space. Let the space become nothing more than a white blinding light that obliterates all that is behind it. When the light disintegrates, all will be emptiness again. When you open your eyes, the negative experience will be dissolved.

People have various experiences finding their guide and sanctuary. For some it's easy; others have difficulty. At first you may doubt the validity of your perceptions, which is understandable since this is an unfamiliar mode of consciousness for most people. Try not to judge what you see. With the proper help and some patience everyone succeeds at it and finds comfort. The following examples show how people in the Process experienced their guide and sanctuary. Janice begins by describing her sanctuary.

> It's a vast meadow, brilliantly alive with wild flowers of the most vivid kind—especially California poppies, in bright orange, and the blues of small cornflowers. There are also myriad tiny white flowers on the meadow. It

stretches almost limitlessly and is sheltered by huge Alpine mountains; they have some trees on them, but above the timberline they are rather a deep maroon color, towering majestically, but not forbidding. I am surprised by the sense of light and the smell of the air. The light is warm and alive, the sky is a brilliant intense blue, the temperature is balmy but somehow brisk, and the air has an invigorating quality to it. A kind of electric joy emanates from the place. It is brilliantly but peacefully alive—open yet sheltered.

A brilliant disc of light appears, and gradually a form begins to appear. Hair first—dark black, coiled in a heavy top knot; a large and serene forehead, shapely brows, and the most limpid amber-colored (brown-yellow) eyes I have ever seen. They look like eyes that understand suffering and have compassion. They seem somewhat sad. Very delicate features—a straight nose and rounded chin, slender neck held regally erect. The rest of the body materializes. I see her as a Hindu Indian woman whose limbs are supple, with lovely, shapely hands, and long, unpolished nails. She is tall, perhaps a little taller than I, regal, and rounded without being at all plump. She has a beautiful, shapely bosom, draped in the folds of her sari, which is of gauzy stuff, deep green with a rosy-red border. She has golden sandals on her feet.

We touch each other's hands, and she smiles, transforming that slightly pensive air to radiance. Her name is Lokani. I feel that she is slightly older than I, enough, say, to have been an older sister; not old enough to be my mother. I don't feel at all jealous or competitive with her, even though she is far more beautiful and graceful than I. She loves me and protects me. She wishes no harm to me. She leads me to a pool made by a stream. We undress and bathe in the pool together. Although it is sun-dappled and partly in the shade, the water is warm and smells of pine and balsam, and we sport in the pool like children. I am delightfully surprised by her playfulness. It is as if suddenly we were both much younger, and I am the playful loving child I was never allowed to be, laughing and playing tag, dashing into the water. Although we are both nude and admire each other's bodies, there is nothing sexual in this context. Lokani hands me a towel and dries my back. She dresses and hands me a sari much like hers except it is deep blue (a color I like) with a rosy border, and we walk off back to the fields again, touching hands occasionally.

We talk very little. She calls me Janice but says, "Sometimes I will call you the name I have given you: Jatma. That will be our special name for when we meet here." She smiles and shows brilliantly white teeth. Her English is beautiful and cultivated, with only the slightest trace of Indian accent. She has been educated abroad. I don't know yet much about who she was or what she did, but I know instinctively she is very wise, that she is especially wise about men, that she has great dignity and serenity, and yet withal, this surprising sense of play. She can go from being a kind of woodsprite to being a queen without any disjunction or confusion. She embodies all these things, so she is always herself in whatever face she presents.

When I tried to pull off her face, she at first reached a hand up as if to defend herself and then took it away to permit me to test her if I must. But I got the sense that my pulling at her face hurt—it was a real face.

Her inability to pull off the guide's face proves that Janice had met her real guide. Had the face been a mask, the guide would have been an impostor. If you get an impostor, it is important to send it away emphatically. There must be no doubt that your sanctuary is completely free of negative forces and totally controlled by you and the nurturing spirit of your guide.

Some people find false guides that are projections of their current concerns or problems. Your real guide is never someone you know or a famous person.

Above all, your guide is supportive and nurturing in a wise, loving way. Betty entered the process with many problems, among them a great deal of self-consciousness and embarrassment about her appearance. She wrote:

My guide was a man and very fair, with a kind of light radiating out from his body all around. He seemed all golden and white . . . robed in white with the gold aura about it. His name is Roan or Rowen. I know I can trust him and that he is all for me and only for good. Here is a dialogue I had with him.

Roan: Here in the sanctuary everything that you will and

wish with your heart and intellect can come to pass. I can see you as the diamond you are. The negativity falls away under my gaze, and to me you are perfect.

BETTY: That is hard for me to imagine, that you see through the crap as if it wasn't there. It is all too much to me. It feels like I am carrying around excess weight. And you don't think my negativities are my fault and that I'm inadequate and hopeless?

ROAN: (Laughs with the sound of wind chimes) Stop that! You can trust my love, and you can trust that whom I love is really there. The radiance that you are, I can see and you will learn to see, too. Just wait and it will all come clear to you. I am here to help you reach that perfect point and then to stay there in clear focus.

Her guide reassured her and helped strengthen the positive within her.

Head trippers at first sometimes have difficulty getting the guide and seeing with their inner eye. Once they learn to turn off their intellects temporarily to allow other parts of their mental abilities to come through, the results can be surprising. "It was hard to see the guide at first," wrote Al, a brilliant young attorney.

Hair and forehead would not jell behind the white disc. They kept changing from a woman's forehead with long brown hair to a man's with strong brow and "butch" haircut. Finally resolved into another naked woman, but with features: taut cheeks, narrow eyes, long face—tense and tough looking. I did not like or trust her, so pulled the face away. Very difficult.

Finally it came off, and there was my friend Marcel, a man. That would not do. I had to pull again. After much searching, my guide turned out to be an old Jewish rabbi, some long-dead ancestor from the seventeenth century named Zev. He seemed incongruous in my Alpine meadow, in his black caftan and black hat. I did not like or trust him instantly, but after a moment I began to feel his solidity. His face was amorphous, somewhat variable. We touched hands, embraced. That helped. He was silent.

The next day Al added this postscript to his guide and sanctuary work:

> AL: You mean this crap that Bob's talking about really is real?
>
> ZEV: It is, it really is.
>
> AL: It is possible through these doors to move toward harmony not only within myself but with nature/vibrations/God/spirit. The experience comes and goes, but when it is with me, it is an incredibly vivid, strong, and personally real vision of how things can be.

Surprise is often a good sign in the guide and sanctuary mind revelation. It shows that you didn't invent or create what you are seeing, which is exactly the point of Al's notes. You cannot create your guide; you can only be receptive to who and what is there. Here is how a student named Robert learned this for himself.

> My interest, so far, is to let the mind revelations flow. My guide is someone named Joseph. He has mixed gray-black-white hair, scraggly, reaching a little below his shoulders. As the disc was descending in front of my guide, I was hoping for a beautiful, warm woman, but this man with his head tilted slightly down appeared. Even though I tried to change him, or replace him with a woman, he steadfastly, stoically, lovingly remained in space and wouldn't budge.

Once you're in the psychic realm, you see what is there for you, not what you want to be there. It's impossible to project. A dialogue can be just like a person-to-person conversation.

> GUIDE: Since you believe in me, why don't you like the way I look? Why do you fight this image of me?
>
> NATALIE: I guess you look a little like a "jock"—those mindless pretty athletes. I've never had much in common with them. And you're blond! I don't usually respond to blonds. I can't really feel they have an intellect.
>
> GUIDE: Ah, the old intellect game. You still want the intellect in the old sense—even though you really do know how limited that is. There's knowing and there's KNOWING.

Don't concern yourself with mind games. The real KNOWING doesn't need those explanations.

NATALIE: OK. Level with me. Who's *really* talking now, you or me?

GUIDE: You know. (He smiles.)

Whatever you see and hear, don't be in awe of your guide. He or she is there to help you. The guide is like a wise, loving friend with whom you can take a peaceful stroll through a beautiful setting whenever you need a release from stress or the answer to a problem. The guide also serves as a model for you while you learn how to love. Your guide loves you, accepts you, despite your negativity, because your guide sees beneath the encrusted surface dirt down to the diamond beneath. If you want to see how loving and acceptance work, simply talk to your guide and see what happens. Develop the habit of talking mentally with your guide. The more you do, the more he or she can help you. As you learn to work with your guide, you will derive knowledge and sustenance. Here is how one young man, smarting over the pain of rejection, used his guide to help him through it.

HOWARD: Somebody whom I wanted to be close with didn't want to be close with me.

GUIDE: Why not?

HOWARD: She said I was too negative, that I wasn't where she was or what she needed. She said call back in two years.

GUIDE: Why does that bother you?

HOWARD: It hurts very much to be told you're not good enough.

GUIDE: Is that what she said?

HOWARD: Not in those words, but that's what it means, doesn't it?

GUIDE: Not necessarily. Maybe the problem is hers, not yours. Maybe she's pushing you away to avoid an emotional involvement she's not mature enough to sustain. Maybe she's rejecting you to avoid being rejected herself. A lot of superior-seeming people do that.

HOWARD: How do I know which it is?

GUIDE: Does it really matter?

HOWARD: God, this all hurts, to think how I blew it. How

I had no choice but to blow it. I fell hard for her and was terribly lonely and couldn't help showing both to her.

GUIDE: (Putting arm around Howard's shoulder) It's all right to show people how you feel.

HOWARD: But knowing that doesn't make the hurt go away.

GUIDE: No, the hurt is part of this experience for you. You see what happened as hurtful, so it inevitably is. Until you understand what it means to have someone say "No" to you, it will always be hurtful.

HOWARD: What do I do now?

GUIDE: Stop chasing after people who don't want or can't see what you have to offer. It's *her* loss, not yours.

With his guide's help this man was able to handle the pain of his rejection pattern.

Beyond helpful advice or information, the guide and sanctuary are useful in temporarily relieving other negative situations that trouble your mind. Here's another way to use this psychic tool. Go to your sanctuary and think of the situation that disturbs you. It may be a personal trait in yourself or a troubling relationship at home or at work. Whatever it is, give it a title, such as PROCRASTINATION or MY BOSS BOTHERS ME.

Now see the negative situation spelled out in large black letters in the space in front of you. See your guide giving you a large, clear plastic bag. While you hold it open, your guide reaches up and one by one plucks the black letters from the ether and drops them into the bag. When all the letters are in the bag, he ties it tightly. The letters are wildly jumping around in the bag, trying to get back into your sanctuary, your mind, to bother you. The negative situation wants to distress you further, but the power of your guide keeps it confined.

Your guide holds out his or her hands. There are white laser beams protruding from the guide's fingertips. The light encircles the bag and withdraws all the energy from it. The letters fall to the bottom of the bag, where they die. The white light intensifies and dissolves the letters into a fine white powder. Your guide opens the bag and pours out the powder. As it hits the earth, wild flowers of all colors sprout from the ground and spell out the positive opposite of the negative situation. PRO-

CRASTINATION has become PUNCTUALITY. Kneel down, smell and caress these lovely flowers.

To heighten the effectiveness of this process, see yourself reliving the same scene and responding to it positively. Instead of procrastinating, for example, see yourself arriving on time feeling relaxed. Experience yourself feeling peaceful about the scene and the situation. You can use this type of "recycling" mind revelation as often as you need help to deal with negative situations. Here's how a woman in the Process used this mind revelation to help herself deal with her jealousy.

> I see my JEALOUSY angrily struggling in the sack and then miraculously stilled and then dissolved by the white light of God. The energy force field of the negativity is withdrawn from the bag by the beam, and the dust remaining in the sack is lifeless and gray. But (will wonders never cease?) this powder, sprinkled on the earth, fertilizes the earth, and up spring wildflowers of every color and fragrance. The negative is recycled into a positive. I see the words SECURE LOVE spelled out in the blossoms. Then I see myself at home waiting for my husband to arrive for dinner. I know that he cares for me and is faithful. I feel secure and confident that he is on his way home to me. I smile to myself with the anticipation of his arrival. I am awed by this process. My jealousy is gone, and what remains is even more faith in the powers of my guide. I feel cleansed and refreshed, as I did when he bathed me in the pure spring waters of the brook.

A woman who was having difficulty on her job had a similar experience. As she used the recycling technique daily, she found not only that her work was improving but so were her relations with her supervisor. Seeing the negative situation being transformed into a positive one has a temporary, beneficial effect and can help you cope with the problem.

Your guide can also help you in dealing with a negative person. Think of someone in your life whom you don't like but must deal with. . . . Have your guide bring the person into your sanctuary. . . . Your guide tells you there's a negative and positive aspect of the person. See your guide separate the positive and negative so the two aspects are standing side by side. . . .

You see the negative, hostile, angry, fearful, or indifferent part of this person. . . . The guide firmly ejects this part from the sanctuary and bars the doors behind it. . . . The negative part of the person tries to get back into your sanctuary by pounding on the doors, but to no avail. There is no way the negative aspect of this person can re-enter your sanctuary. It has no choice but to walk down the tunnel to the outside where his own guide awaits to give him succor. Then you turn toward the positive part of this person. You may be surprised at what you see. Greet him. Allow yourself to see this positive person as his real essence no matter how deeply covered by the negative personality you have just removed. Permit his positive side to rejoin his negative side and his guide outside the tunnel. Practice this mind revelation as often as necessary to cleanse your mind and spirit of the negative people that bug you.

To rid yourself temporarily of blocks or other negativities, you can use the following mind revelation. See your guide holding a large syringe. Your guide puts the end gently against your skin and painlessly withdraws a dark, ugly fluid. As the syringe fills, a label appears on it with the name of the negativity. (Often it's something like DEFENSIVENESS.) After that first vial is filled, your guide hurls it into the air, where it explodes into cosmic dust. He or she then fills another, and then keeps withdrawing the negative fluid from you until there is no more inside.

Next your guide takes a syringe filled with a pure white, luminous serum, which is the antithesis of your negativity and injects your Trinity with this restorative fluid. . . . Feel it flow throughout your Trinity. . . . Experience the warmth and vibrance that comes from removing a negative feeling and replacing it with a positive, affirmative feeling. See your spirit filled with the positive beauty it needs to reprogram your brain. . . . Use this ejection-injection mind revelation as often as you like to help you deal with the blocks and resistances that keep you from being your complete, most realized self.

A 38-year-old housewife used this mind revelation to help her deal with stresses at home. "I feel that I must keep some sort of balance around my children. I tried ejecting UPSET and IRRITATION and injecting SERENITY and KINDNESS just before they came home from school one day, and it made me feel better and more able to cope with them, so now I do it every morning before I wake them up and again in the afternoon. It really helps!" (The permanent help came when she learned to love herself after the Process.)

Here's how a 21-year-old woman used this mind revelation.

> I was at home last Saturday evening and feeling sort of blue. I knew it was because I had broken up with Ken a couple of weeks before, and I didn't have a date that night, but I got thinking that it really wasn't right to feel so down about it. So I had my guide withdraw a big syringe full of LONELINESS from my arm. When he threw it up in the air, and it exploded, I didn't feel much different, but he came right back and took out another one, and then another one. I hadn't realized that I was so full of my own loneliness, but it took three syringes to get it all out. Then he injected a big, warm, glowing syringe full of GOOD FEELINGS. I could actually feel them spreading throughout my body, and right away I thought about my macramé I hadn't had time to finish, and I started to feel cheerful. I got it out and had a really good time completing it.
>
> I've got to tell you that the next morning I still felt good when I met my friend Sherry to go hiking, and we met a couple of really nice guys on our hike, and I've got a date for next Saturday night!

The ejection-injection mind revelation can be especially helpful in recalling forgotten incidents from childhood. Have your guide use the syringe to withdraw I CAN'T REMEMBER. Continue withdrawing it until you are completely empty of defensive forgetting. Then your guide injects into your Trinity the pure white fluid of EXCELLENT MEMORY RECALL. You will find that even a few repetitions of this mind revelation will help you enormously in recalling many details from the past.

The sanctuary is also the place in which mind-cleansing takes place. Years ago, I worked with a 13-year-old boy who was still wetting the bed almost every night. His bed wetting had continued long after most children stop because of his desperate need for attention, even negative attention. His parents were giving all their positive attention to his older sister, and he couldn't compete with her. Out of rebellion he continued to disobey his parents' admonition to sleep through the night. To lend credence to his sleeplessness, he began to imagine monsters in the dark that frightened him. There is a fine line of demarcation between the realm of imagination and the psychic realm of the mind. Negative psychic forces took over, and he soon found himself feeling possessed by demonlike figures that frightened him every night, causing his brain to produce terrifying visions that made him lose control of his bladder. In his angry rebellion he created a device for gaining negative attention that evolved into a frightening emotional problem.

In working with him I gave him the "guide and sanctuary" mind revelation. He was then able to go to his sanctuary each night before going to sleep. Together he and his guide ushered the frightening visions out of his sanctuary and out of his mind. Once his mind was cleansed of the negative forces, he automatically stopped wetting the bed. While the guide and sanctuary were enough to rid him of the bed wetting, by themselves they are not enough to de-program completely the negative love syndrome. The entire Fischer-Hoffman Process is needed for complete mind cleansing.

Above all, the guide and sanctuary are designed to enhance and support your postive loving self, but the guide and sanctuary are not merely a form of positive thinking. "Think positively" or "It's all in your mind" are just admonitions that create further conflict. Negativity remains until it is removed through reprogramming, and the mind revelations are some of our tools to accomplish this.

Nor does the Process involve admonitions to "Be more loving!" How can anyone obey such a command when mother and father, the two most important persons in anyone's life, didn't teach love? Without the childhood experience of love, or the love training of the Process, such an admonition just yields more conflict and inner distress. The remainder of this book describes the highlights of the Process itself and how it is possible to eradicate negative love patterns.

5. Hostile, Baygull, or Zombie?

Most people show themselves to the world in one of three ways: Hostile, Baygull, or Zombie. The Hostiles are just what they appear to be: angry, gruff, difficult to approach, and hard to please. They are easy to spot.

In direct contrast to the overt Hostile is the Baygull, full of false good humor and phony spirituality. (The term Baygull comes from a 1973 *New York Times* photo satirizing Richard Bach's *Jonathan Livingston Seagull.* The photo introduces a bird named Wellington Goldfarb Baygull. While flying high above the bay, lost in the spirituality of the great gullness of Either/Or, he hit a fence projecting from the shore and plopped into the bay.) The Baygulls are goody-goodies who appear to be loving but actually feel no love either for themselves or others. They are easier to get along with than the Hostiles, since they rarely fight or disagree, but their smiles are only a mask to cover unloved emptiness. The Baygull man or woman uses surface pleasantness to drain others dry of love while giving only pseudo-love in return. Like the others, they give only to get.

Between the scowl of the Hostile and the smile of the Baygull is the blank expression of the Zombie. He is the one who goes unnoticed in the crowd by showing no emotion, positive or negative. The Zombie is the drab, lifeless person whose name you have the toughest time remembering because he's not fully "there" in any situation.

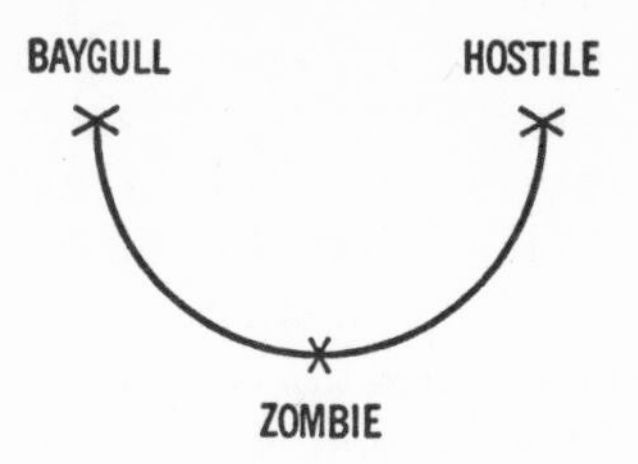

Taken together, the Hostile, Baygull, and Zombie types make up the Rocky Arc of Emotion (Fig. 1). Most people rock back and forth on the emotional arc, depending on the situation, but they tend to have a favorite face they show the world. Rocking back and forth creates much confusion and emotional instability. To discover your place on the Rocky Arc, consider the following two exercises.

Imagine yourself at age twenty-one in the following scenes. A young man spending his lunch hour in the park meets a young woman doing the same. They speak together, like each other, and begin dating. They have sex together and enjoy it. After a few weeks, he invites her to have a gourmet dinner at his apartment. When she arrives for dinner, she is pleasantly surprised at his tidy apartment and his refusal to let her help. She gives him a bottle of fine wine she has brought as a gift. He kisses her tenderly and thanks her for her thoughtfulness. Offering her a seat on the sofa, he brings her a cocktail, hors d'oeuvres, and sits beside her while they chat happily. Dinner is timed correctly, and at 7:30 he seats her at the table. There is no awkwardness or wasted energy. He uncorks the wine she has brought and serves a great meal, with all her favorite foods expertly prepared. She is amazed and delighted by his culinary skill. Each time he leaves to serve another course, he kisses her and tells her to sit still, he can do it himself. When dinner is completed, he says pleasantly, "You've had a tough day, darling. Go sit on the sofa and read a magazine. It won't take me long to clean up the dishes and the kitchen. I'll be with you shortly."

You are the guest. (Male readers should reverse the roles so that it is the woman who cooks for the male guest.) What would you do in this situation? Make a note of how you would respond before reading the next story.

This situation is similar to the first story. The two young people have been dating for a short time, and the woman says to him, "Why don't you come over for dinner tomorrow night at 6:30? I enjoy cooking." (If you are a woman, reverse the roles so he is cooking for you.) He thinks this is a great idea and arrives the next evening dressed in his best casual outfit. He brings a bottle of her favorite wine.

When he arrives at her apartment on time, he finds the door ajar. He walks in and smells something burning in the kitchen. The apartment is unkempt. Nylons and a girdle are on the sofa. The place appears not to have been cleaned in months. No table is set. She's talking on the telephone with a girlfriend, rehashing a party they had been to the week before. She holds her hand over the mouthpiece, says she will be with him in a few minutes, and asks him to make the drinks. After about ten minutes she hangs up the phone. She takes the drink and sits in a chair across from him rather than on the sofa next to him. Then her complaints begin. "What a lousy day I had," she groans. On and on she goes about her horrible boss, how everything went wrong, and how tired she is. The phone rings again, and it's another man inviting her for a date the next weekend. As she laughs and jokes with the caller, she turns to her guest and says, "The dishes are in the cabinet in the dining room. Do you mind setting the table? I'll be with you in a few minutes." Then she continues her phone conversation.

He gets up, finds the dishes, which have been unused for a long time, and manages to wipe the grime off them and set some sort of table. When the hostess gets off the phone, she continues with her drink. The phone rings again, and it's her mother, with whom she launches into a long, unpleasant harangue. The guest is left sitting alone. He waits to see what will develop. Eventually she returns to him and says, "Well, let's have dinner." She serves a horrible meal. The soup is watery, the roast is burned, the potatoes are cold and lumpy. Then she says, "You didn't want any dessert, did you?" (She knows he loves desserts.) She adds, "I've stopped drinking coffee, and you should stop, too." So no coffee is served, although he likes coffee very much. Soon she yawns and says, "Gee, I'm so tired. I'm going to lie down for a few minutes. Do you mind doing the dishes for me?"

What would you do as the guest? Make a note of your gut-level response to this story before reading on.

How people respond to these short stories shows where they are on the Rocky Arc. The host or hostess in the stories represents your parents and their treatment of you. The guest's reactions show how you responded to their positive and negative treatment, and how you are continuing to react even now. The loving response to the first story would be to return the warm devotion you have received by gently persuading your host that you wish to continue being together and share the work. To respond this way shows that when mother and father treated you well as a child, you responded in kind.

There is no love in the second story. The self-loving response to the host's mistreatment is to withdraw calmly as soon as the situation becomes apparent, while feeling neither guilty for taking care of yourself nor angry for the unexpected turn of events. Such healthy emotional responses are rare, because of our negative programming. We respond to the world as we learned to respond to our parents during our childhood.

To demonstrate this, the following sample responses to the two dinner stories come from the notes of three persons in the Fischer-Hoffman Process. The responses are used as quick, simple tools for determining one's basic emotional attitude toward himself and his parents and his place on the Rocky Arc.

"What would I do?" wrote Nancy, a 27-year-old executive secretary who is a Hostile. "I'd let 'golden boy' do the dishes while I rested. I wouldn't be at all comfortable about it, but he's so good at handling everything that I'd probably just get in his way if I insisted on helping."

Her sarcasm and hostility are evident from the beginning of Nancy's answer. When mother and father treated her well, she obeyed, although she quickly turned it into an excuse to put down both them and herself. To the second, highly negative story she wrote, "I'd like to say that I'd have poured the dishwater over the selfish jerk. But I'd probably have just walked out, too angry to say anything at all to him."

When Nancy was treated badly as a child, she rebelled by sulking and going off by herself. Although she knows there's no love available, she dares not vent her anger for fear of losing in a confrontation.

In contrast to Nancy's hostility is the Zombie response of Chris, a 46-year-old psychologist.

"My first reaction (to the offer to rest while the hostess cleans up after dinner) is 'Great. Thanks. I'll wait on the couch.' My second reaction is to volunteer to help her, a probably enjoyable experience for both of us."

His terse comments and lack of emotion are typical of Zombies, who are giving the minimum to others while holding themselves in. To the second, highly negative story he wrote:

"My first reaction is, 'No, I won't do the dishes alone. But if we do them together, it'll get done fast.' With any encouragement I would explain how her actions have made me feel: hurt, uncared for, used, and cheated."

Here Chris shifts somewhat toward Baygull obedience. He's following her lead instead of taking the initiative against her abuse of him. He rebels by refusing to do the dishes alone, but quickly retreats from it and covers it with an offer of appeasement. He's still hoping he can win her around to giving him some show of love despite her already clear rejection of him.

On the other end of the Rocky Arc is Laura, a thirty-five-year-old real estate saleswoman. She's a Baygull with latent Hostile tendencies.

> What's my reaction? I would have sat down as he suggested. But instead of relaxing, I would have tried to figure out how I felt about him. What kind of "after dinner entertainment" did he want? Did I want to go to bed with him? Mostly my thought would be on trying to puzzle out whether he was expecting it as his reward, in which case I wouldn't do it.
>
> In the second story I would have tried valiantly to make a plausible excuse to leave or escape, always smiling and being very polite but angry and resentful. I'm afraid I might have stayed to do the dishes, though, as long as I was fairly sure he wouldn't try to maul me to complete the rotten evening.

Her response to the dinner stories shows that Laura was so manipulated as a child that she cannot respond to the loving treatment in the first story except with suspicion and confusion. She cannot believe anyone would be nice to her except with an ulterior motive. The story specifically states they were already having sex, but she still worries about it. By doing what her host tells her, she shows she was an obedient child when her parents treated her well. The second story shows that no matter how badly she was treated, she would stick around with a fake smile on her face, hoping for a crumb of love. Her angry rebellion was covered by her need to maintain a pleasant appearance at all costs.

Where are you on the Rocky Arc of Emotion? Are you the angry Hostile, the smiling Baygull, or the emotionally dead Zombie? Perhaps you are some combination of the three, rocking dizzily back and forth. Your response to the two stories shows not only your place on the Arc, but how you responded to the kind of programming you received as a child.

The negative love programming is only yours by adoption; you can learn to drop it. The first step toward freedom is to see how and when you adopted it from your parents during your first thirteen years of life.

Learning to love in the Fischer-Hoffman Process requires a series of six stages. The first stage is the Prosecution of Mother, in which you recall and relive emotionally the anger for the wrongs she did to you. It is a complete, overwhelmingly intense purging of every bit of negative feeling toward mother lying unexpressed within you since childhood.

The second stage, the Defense of Mother, holds an equally important truth. Mother was once a child herself and was also programmed. Knowing this intellectually isn't enough to break the grip of the programming. It must be seen and experienced emotionally in order to arrive at a truly compassionate understanding of mother's tragedy of lovelessness. With emotional understanding and no condemnation, mother is absolved, and the childhood hostility to her disappears. After the Defense of Mother, it becomes possible to begin dropping her negativities and replacing them with positive patterns.

The same two-stage procedure is used with father. He, too, must first be prosecuted for his sins of omission and commission. It is impossible to defend him truly until he has first been thoroughly prosecuted for his part in the negative love programming. Once the anger is spent, though, he appears as just another programmed little boy grown old but not up. His defense, like mother's, requires seeing and emotionally experiencing how he was an unwitting victim of the negative love syndrome and helplessly passed the disease along to his children. After his defense, his negative traits begin to lose their grip and can be recycled to their positive opposites. (Those with step-parents, foster parents, or other relatives who brought them up must have more than one prosecution and defense.)

The four stages of the Prosecution and Defense of Mother and Father effectively turn people inside out. After ending the war with the parents, it is time to end the war between the negative emotional child and the intellect. When you find yourself thinking one way while acting another, you are experiencing the effects of this internal conflict. This fifth stage of the Process consists of a confrontation between the present-day intellect and the negative emotional child. They vent their mutual hostility, work through it, and reach a state of truce.

The final resolution of all internal conflict and the reintegration of the fragmented Quadrinity take place in the sixth stage, known as Closure. It is a re-birthday. The divorce from mother and father finally becomes a loving one, allowing your true, mature self to emerge. Closure is the ultimate goal toward which the entire Process is directed.

The Prosecution of Mother begins with recalling her negative traits and the incidents in which she expressed them. In the Process we use a list of negative traits, moods, and admonitions to help clients clarify their thoughts and recollections about mother's negativity. The entire list runs to several hundred different traits, moods, and admonitions, both silent and overt, clustered under more than a dozen major headings. For example, under the cluster heading Uncaring/Nonsupportive are dozens of such specifics as:

1. Cold
2. Neglectful
3. Not loving
4. Insensitivity in relationships
5. Non-supportive
6. Inconsiderate
7. Stingy
8. Selfish
9. Disrespect toward spouse and children

10. Moods: I don't have time for you.
    I am more important than you.
11. Admonitions: Your feelings are not important.
    Children should be seen and not heard.
    Don't tell me your troubles.

The general negative love patterns described in Chapter 2 are composed of how we respond to specific traits such as these, whether we adopt them or rebel against them. It is not unusual to find as many as several hundred traits, moods, and admonitions that mother displayed during your childhood. Each is a potential source of adult despair and unhappiness. (Father's traits are the other source of negativity but are not considered until the mother work is completed. If mother's and father's traits are incompatible, this conflict in itself is another cause of confusion and emotional instability.)

In the next chapter we will present the Mother Prosecution work of three clients: Nancy (a Hostile), Chris (a Zombie), and Laura (a Baygull). Their own natural sensory perception abilities plus some further mind revelations enabled them to answer many early life questions. Clients who later check out what they have sensed are usually amazed at the high level of accuracy of their psychic receptions. In order to do their work with full impact, they first had to become aware of the different kinds of mothering and recognize their own particular deprivations. Their eyes were opened by the following rude questions.

Did your mother want you? How did she feel about being pregnant? How did she feel about your father during her pregnancy with you? Their own natural sensory perception abilities plus some further mind revelations enabled them to answer early life questions. Clients who later check out what they have sensed are usually amazed at the high level of accuracy of their psychic receptions. Were you the sex mother wanted? If not, mother may have pushed you away, felt guilty about the rejection, and then smothered you with compensatory guilt love to hide her true feelings about you. If you are the wrong sex in mother's eyes, her invalidation and rejection of you began the day you were born.

Did you feel *really* loved by mother? Or did she treat you as another burden, when she already had too much to handle? Did she ignore you or relegate your upbringing to older children or other relatives? Was she there when you needed her until your puberty? If she died or deserted you before your puberty, she cheated you of your right to a consistent flow of mother's love. The child within you is still angry with mother for leaving, whatever the cause or explanation. *She left, and you lost a mother's love.*

How did mother show you her love? Did she take time from her schedule to spend a few quiet moments with you? Or was she so absorbed in her own activities that you felt you were intruding if you sought her attention? Did she greet you with a hug and kiss when you came through the door? Or was she off pursuing her selfish interests? It is defensive to say, "I know she loved me even if she had trouble showing it." *When do you remember being held lovingly in her arms?* There's a difference between intellectually believing you're loved and *feeling* that love surround you. If you *believe* but don't *feel* that she loved you, you may well suspect that she was play-acting at the role of loving mother, offering only pseudo-love.

How did mother teach you to relate to your brothers and sisters? Did she teach you to compete with all the others for the few crumbs of attention and affection she doled out? Was mother able to ease you lovingly through the transition period after the arrival of a younger child? Or were you abruptly displaced in favor of your younger brother or sister? Part of mother's responsibility is to prepare each child for the arrival of the next by including, not excluding, the older ones. The horror of sibling rivalry is not inevitable or natural. It is the direct result of mother's failure to create a loving atmosphere in which each child feels united with the others and with her.

Some mothers truly believe they prepare the older child for the younger child's birth, but it is rarely successful. To prevent the emotionally crippling experience of sibling rivalry, mother has to be a loving woman and a loving mother who is able to give for the sake of giving. Picture the following:

Mother is pregnant, and you are an only child. She takes you in her motherly arms and says, "Ron, *we're* going to have a baby! *We* are going to have a baby." She doesn't say, "I am going to have a baby," or, "Your father and I are going to have a baby." She says *we.* This includes Ron. She doesn't say, "You're going to have a brother." If Ron asks, "What's it going to be, Mom?" the mother answers, "It is going to be a boy or a girl, whatever God gives us. *We* will love it." Again, *we* will love it. Mother lets Ron feel her abdomen as the fetus grows. He feels the baby kick. With this preparation and mother's constant love, all goes well until the birth.

After mother enters the hospital to give birth, father should tell the child, "Mother's in the hospital. She's only going to be gone a few days, and Aunt Ellen is here to help us. When mother comes home, she'll bring *our baby* with her. *We* have a baby sister for you. She's very pretty, and you'll love her. Her name is Katherine Louise."

Aunt Ellen takes loving care of Ron. When Daddy is home he does as much as he can to let the child know that he is loved, cared for, and wanted. Ron is repeatedly reminded that the baby in the hospital with mommy is *our baby.* A few days later, when the infant is ready to be brought home, a nurse or friend is asked to hold the infant outside the home while mother and dad enter. Mother exclaims, "Where's my little Ron? Oh, Ron, there you are! Oh, mommy loves you and missed you so! Come here, darling." Ron runs to mother, receiving affection in her arms. He is happy to see her because she makes him feel loved, comforted, and secure. She transmits feelings of mother love, acceptance, and approval. The child then remembers the baby and asks, "Where is our baby?" Mother replies, "Oh, yes! We have a baby sister." The baby is then brought in and when first seen by Ron is not in mother's or father's arms. Jealousy is avoided. When the baby is brought in, mother is holding Ron on her lap. The friend or nurse then places the baby on Ron's lap while mother holds both of them. Mother doesn't touch the baby. Ron is holding *his* sister. Mother caresses Ron in her arms, kissing him, fondling him, and making statements like, "Isn't our baby cute? It's our baby, sweetheart. You can kiss our baby if you want to. It's okay." The older child kisses "our" baby. Mother has transferred love to the older child and he to the baby. This continues for a while. Ron perhaps plays with the baby's tiny fingers and toes. Since he has been receiving love from mother, he doesn't feel rejected, and he is not angry and resentful of the infant. It becomes a joyous project, taking care of *our* infant. Mother might ask, "Shall we put *our* baby to sleep? Would you like to rock *our* baby?" Variations of this scene continue for a few days.

Note that all this time mother gives love and affection to

the first child as she did before the birth of the baby. He does not feel rejected. The baby is also not feeling rejected, for its older sibling transfers mother's love to it. One day soon, however, something like this will happen. Ron comes over to mommy after he has kissed and loved *our* baby and realizes, for the first time, that mother hasn't kissed *our* baby, and he says to mother, indignantly, "Mommy, you kiss our baby, too!" *Now* mommy has permission to kiss, to fondle, to be affectionate, and to love *our* baby. She shares this love equally with the baby and her older son. No sibling rivalry can or will occur if she follows this pattern throughout the child-rearing days. Parents who have used it report this process is highly successful in preventing the scars of sibling rivalry.

Unfortunately, what usually happens after a baby is born is something like this: The baby is brought home in mother's arms and becomes the new center of attention. The next older child turns away, filled with jealousy, anger, and insecurity. He is no longer number one, and his replacement is occupying *his* rightful place. Or, if he is programmed for goody-goody obedience, he may outwardly accept the baby while sulking and avenging his anger by secretly mistreating the infant when mother is away or not looking. The angel's halo often turns to devil's horns when the opportunity presents itself. If being nice to the younger one appears to be the way to get mother's love, he may hide his frustration and resentment behind a façade of sweetness and affection. The internal conflict remains for life.

The apparent triumph of the second child turns to emotional catastrophe if a third child appears. He loses his favored status but finds no warmth from his older brother, who continues to resent him. He in turn resents the youngest. He is sandwiched between them and often has no one to whom he can turn. The middle child is often put into a terrible position. The first and third children may get along well together, however, since they are usually not rivals. The ones next in line to each other have great difficulties developing mutual love and trust unless mother has enough love for each of them, which rarely happens.

If you had an older brother or sister, recall what it was like. Were you loving friends, or hostile enemies? If the next older child was a brother, perhaps you wanted to be loved and accepted by him, but he only played with you until friends his own age came around. Then he ignored you, teased or bullied you. While you may have been hurt and resentful toward your brother or sister, the cruel treatment was really mother's fault. Had she prepared the older one properly for your arrival and not slighted her or him after your birth, the tragedy of sibling rivalry could have been avoided. Your older sister or brother was as much a victim as you were. Each of you lost out on the experience of brotherly love because of mother's ineptness.

What was your first day of school like? Did mother help you prepare for this new adventure by opening you to the thrill of learning? Or did she see school as a way to get rid of you for a few hours while she attended to your younger rivals at home? Did she take you to school and warmly reassure you that you weren't being abandoned to hostile strangers? Did she really care about what you were doing in school? How did she respond when you brought home a treasured piece of work for her approval? Later, when you brought home report cards, how did she treat you? Was she indifferent to your progress? Did she always criticize without adding any praise for achievement? Did she make you feel like a failure if you weren't first in the class? Did she expect you to perform well so that she could advance herself in the eyes of her friends? Did she come to school on parents day?

How did your mother handle the special days of the year, such as your birthday, Christmas, and other holidays? Were these occasions really joyous and festive? Or did she treat each as a domestic burden to be endured with a false smile? Were these events really family occasions? Or were they semipublic presentations in which mother "proved" what a good mother she was by showing off her household to relatives and neighbors? Was your birthday party for you or for her? Or perhaps she totally ignored your birthday? Were holiday meals prepared and served with love and warmth? Or were they joyless, dutiful affairs? How did she respond to the gifts you gave her?

How did mother discipline you? Did she smack you around at the slightest provocation, teaching you to fear her anger? Or did she ignore your misdeeds and fail to give you clear guidelines for behavior? Did she give you the silent treatment to show her displeasure? Or did she ignore discipline and leave it to your father? Did she have a sense of justice, making the "punishment fit the crime"? Did she help you feel loved even while temporarily withholding a privilege? Or did she teach you to see yourself as a sinner in need of punishment? Did she teach you to be afraid of admitting a mistake? Or did she show you that errors are the natural way we all learn?

A child will always test mother's love through misbehavior. In response, the three basic forms of discipline usually exhibited are: (1) the cast-iron fist of harsh discipline, (2) the limp wrist of indecisive discipline, and (3) the firm hand of loving discipline.

An example of the first discipline, the cast-iron fist, shows mother working in the home. The child wants attention or perhaps wants to get even with mother for loving the baby instead of him. He knocks down one of mother's favorite vases. Mother sees it happen, is furious, and spanks the boy. "You naughty child! Look what you've done! You've broken mother's favorite vase. Go to your room. First give me those comic books. And there's no television for three days! You're a miserable brat!" This is followed by a few more slaps. The child goes to his room and cries, "Mommy doesn't love me, and I hate her, too!" He had tested mother, found her wanting, and now has a legitimate reason to hate her.

If mother follows the limp wrist type of discipline, she will see the broken vase and say in a Zombie tone of voice, "Oh, Ron, why did you do that? Now run along outside and play somewhere else, dear." She then sweeps up the mess and throws it in the garbage. The child is left in limbo. He doesn't know what to expect. The child doesn't know if he's cared for or not because there was no response from mother. He learned that she is a *care-less* mother. He is unimportant. He doesn't count and isn't worthy even of negative attention.

The third and correct way of disciplining a child is with the firm hand of love. When the vase is dropped, mother speaks in a firm but not angry tone of voice, "Ron, you broke my vase purposely." Ron says, "Mom, I didn't mean to." Mother continues in an even tone of voice, "But I saw you do it, Ron." "But, Mom . . ." Mother says, calmly but directly, "I saw you do it, and I love you too much, Son, to permit you to destroy someone else's property. Since you did do it on purpose, you have to accept the consequences of what you've done. Hand me those comic books. There will be no television for three days. Now, go to your room." Ron, whimpering: "Mom, I didn't mean to." Mother, "Oh, but you did do it, and you have to learn right from wrong. But first come here, Son." Mother takes Ron in her arms and says quietly and lovingly, "You have to be punished, and mother loves you." She kisses him and tells him to run along. As Ron goes to his room accepting his just punishment, he smiles to himself. "Mother loves me." He plays in his room until punishment time is over. He is secure in his knowledge of mother's consistent love. He has tested mother and not found her wanting. He learned the difference between right and wrong, with love. Did your mother discipline you this way?

How did she handle your illnesses? Did she make you feel guilty for getting sick and breaking her routine? Or did your illnesses make her anxious and nervous? Did she teach you that getting sick was the only way to get her sympathetic, tender attention? Did she know how to handle your needs with intelligence and understanding? Or did she become confused and helpless?

Mother's attitude toward your father was your first lesson in how women relate to men. Did she respect and understand your father? Did she lovingly greet him when he came home? Did she hold him up to you as a worthy example to emulate? Or did she run him down, criticizing and emasculating him so that you learned women are shrews, and men are no good? Was mother an equal to your father, sharing with him in making important decisions affecting the family? Or was she his frightened victim, obediently taking orders? What example did she set?

How did mother treat your friends? Was she jealous of anyone who took you away from her? Or did she push you away and force other people on you in order to keep you occupied? Did she choose your friends for you, thus teaching you not to trust your own judgment about people? Or did she allow you to choose your own while letting you know she disapproved of your choices? Were certain groups of people unacceptable as potential friends? If so, mother planted the seeds of your adult prejudices.

Did mother have a sense of humor? Was laughter a part of her life? Was she able to see the funny side of herself as well as others? When she laughed, was it with genuine enjoyment and pleasure? Above all, did she teach you how to see the light side of life's inevitable problems and difficulties? Or was she so caught up in anxiety or anger that there was no room for amusement? If mother didn't teach you to laugh, she cheated you of one of life's best free remedies against despair and self-hatred. For that alone she deserves to be prosecuted.

We have already discussed puberty and sex education in detail in Chapter 3. This final stage in your childhood relationship with mother is extremely important, for it propels you toward your adult sexuality. What kind of sendoff did your mother give you? Was she frank without being callous? Did she tenderly give you the information and guidance you needed? Did mother help you celebrate your emergence into adulthood?

The day of your first menstruation or seminal discharge is the second most important day of your life, after the day of your birth. (The third most important day occurs when your body dies.) The onset of puberty marks the end of childhood and its negative love programming. The rest of life is spent replaying the tapes (unless something is done to erase the tapes and make new ones). If mother programmed you negatively about your sexuality, she cheated you of the enjoyment of love's most magnificent physical expression.

In remembering your childhood with mother, keep in mind that her acts of omission are also vital. Often people will say, "Mother never said anything about . . ." Although there may be no painful trauma to be recalled, what she didn't do has thoroughly negative effects. Whatever was missing that would have made for a complete mother-child relationship is evidence against her. If you have difficulty recalling much of your relationship with mother, remember that we tend to forget the painful incidents from the past to protect ourselves. One of the tragedies of negative love patterns is that we continue to live the programming long after forgetting where it came from. It just seems to be part of us. The purpose of recalling mother's negative traits and the scenes in which she expressed them is to remind us that we became our negative selves by emulating her or rebelling against her.

Once the traits are recorded and the scenes are recalled, it is possible to write the story of the childhood relationship with mother from the negative perspective. In the Process we call it the Negative Emotional Autobiography with Mother. Writing out the memories and the emotions attached to them helps clarify the emerging picture of mother as an overwhelmingly negative person who passed along the crud of negative love to her innocent children. Seeing her from this perspective is an important preparation for the emotional outpouring that follows in what we call bitch sessions. Getting through the negative programming requires an overt rebellion against the bitch mother. The hostility must flare up like an exploding volcano. This can't be done just by screaming or ranting, "Poor me! Poor me!" The angry feelings must be directed where they belong: at the mother who failed you in the worst possible way by not providing a consistent flow of nourishing love.

The overt Hostile easily vents his anger during the Prosecution of Mother. He comes into the Process knowing he's angry at everyone, including his parents, without really understanding why. In his hostility he has turned her rejection of him into his rejection of others. With mother's negative trait list and the negative emotional autobiography, he is able to redirect and focus his anger on its real source, his unloving mother.

Some people, particularly the Baygull goody-goodies, say they can't bitch at mother, or later at father, because of the Biblical commandment to "honor thy father and mother." The best way to honor mother and father is by doing for yourself what they were unable to do for you. Once you learn to love yourself and others, you can be a far better son or daughter than you ever will be if you remain chained to them with negative love.

Other people on heavy religious, meditation, or spiritual trips have trouble bitching at mother because they feel they have already forgiven her. Their rationale for holding back their true feelings of anger and contempt for mother amount to something like this: "See, Mother, how I've grown and matured? I'm above all that anger and resentment from the past. I forgave you long ago." Are you *sure* you've forgiven mother?

Or the Baygulls sometimes commiserate with mother: "Poor Mommy. I won't let these people abuse you and put you down this way. I know you tried hard. You won't love me if I let them put you down. So I'll protect you, don't worry." Permitting the client to cling to this self-deception would allow him to lose the war against the effects of his negative love programming. If there is no emotional purging of the anger against mother, there can be no genuine reintegration of the four parts of the Quadrinity. The smiling Baygull must be made to realize that feeling and expressing the anger is the only way to deal with it.

With Zombies, the problem is often even more difficult. They have been programmed to feel nothing. The older and deader they are, the more difficult it is to crack them open so they can bitch at mother. Once open, though, they bitch all the more violently for the years of emotional paralysis.

Whatever the excuse, it must be confronted and demolished. Genuine compassion and understanding with no condemnation, the vital intermediate steps toward learning to love, can only be achieved by first clearing out the festering disease. Again and again this point is driven home until everyone, Hostile, Baygull, and Zombie, understands that the only way to attain peace with mother is to go to war against her in the bitch session.

The bitch session itself is different from the earlier Process sessions. Initially, clients take notes on the information in the lecture, while reserving the expression of their mind revelations and inner experiences for the one-to-one work with their personal teacher. Group meetings are not encounter or discussion groups. Some questions are asked, but the interaction between client and teacher occurs through the written notes, the tape-recorded feedback, and face-to-face sessions when necessary.

On bitch night the anger that will cleanse them of the negative love programming, and give them permission to rebel against it totally, needs to be fully and openly expressed. Individuals are asked to wear comfortable clothing, permitting complete freedom of movement. Each brings a pillow. The group divides into smaller groups of four or five with a facilitator to assist with the bitching. We encourage the use of street language and curse words because they have great shock value and promote gut-level emotional bitching.

At this point, the weeks of work on mother's negative trait list and the negative emotional autobiography pay off. The shock is powerful when everyone is made to see that by adopting her negativities through negative love he or she is that bitch mother all over again. They recognize the source of their lifelong discontent, distress, and misery is none other than the bitch mother who failed them so miserably and with such devastating consequences. After a further mind revelation to prime the anger and intensify the pressure, each is instructed to "put mother on the pillow" and confront her with words, fists, and foam bats.

There is no sound quite like the din of two dozen men and women settling the old scores with mother. With total lack of restraint and animal-like fury, they let her have it for all the lies, put-downs, abuses, injustices, and denials from childhood, including the worst sin of all: not loving. The air is filled with the sounds of a riot: screams, curses, crying, the dull thudding of bats and fists against pillows. Each person is allowed to bitch at mother until his energy is spent. This may take an hour or more. No one is allowed to fail the bitch session and if necessary further help is given. It is crucial that they bitch at mother completely until they break through to uncontrollable, visceral anger.

The bitch session sometimes has its light side despite the heavily charged atmosphere. The afternoon before the bitch session we phone the local police department to inform them that a noisy but harmless session is scheduled for that evening. Once, when my secretary forgot to make the call, we found ourselves in the middle of a bitch session face to face with several officers prepared to make arrests for murder and mayhem! When we explained the procedure, and they satisfied themselves that no one was injured, they left shaking their heads in disbelief.

Following the evening bitch session, clients are advised to take a tape recorder to the woods the next day, find a rock, and chalk mother's picture on it. They throw stones at mother's face while experiencing and taping a second bitch session. This second bitch session reinforces the first and provides further release for the years of pent-up anger and resentment. The tape is later reviewed by the teacher to ensure that the bitching has been done completely and with full intensity.

At a deep level everyone is hostile toward the parents who failed to teach them to love themselves and others. *Everyone!* Once the right button is pressed, anyone will explode. Finding the right button and knowing how to press it is something only a trained teacher can do. Rarely does one confront himself and call his own lies. It hurts too much, and it's too easy to stop looking at the truth when the exposed nerves start throbbing. The procedure is like an operation with no anesthetic, as the notes of Nancy, Chris, and Laura in the next chapter make clear. Each experienced the pain of building to the catharsis of the bitch session against mother but afterward achieved a great sense of relief.

6. "I Hate You, You Bitch!"

These notes are excerpts from the Process work of a Hostile (Nancy), a Zombie (Chris), and a Baygull (Laura). None is a pure type; the notes of each contain fragments characteristic of the others. Nancy, the Hostile, was programmed to suppress her feelings and therefore is sometimes Zombielike, while Chris the Zombie shows some Baygull false pleasantness. Laura's Baygullism, of course, is a cover for deep hostility that only gains expression when she is free to bitch at mother.

The incidents from their childhood emotional autobiographies show the origins of their place on the Rocky Arc of Emotion. The intense feedback each received, presented in summary form here, helped fan the fires of their anger while opening their eyes to the reality of their negative love attachment to mother. As Chris so aptly put it, "I can't believe it! *I am my mother!*" The segments from their subsequent bitch sessions show, once they became free to express it, the fury of their anger.

While the negative emotional autobiography tells the story of the client's childhood relationship with mother, it is not a case history in the usual sense. We do not compile extensive biographical, medical, or psychiatric profiles. Our concern is never with where the clients have been, but with where they are and where they are going. The purpose of the negative emotional autobiography with mother, and later with father, is to show the client how his current negative behavior patterns result directly from the negative patterns of his mother and father. It is not enough to say something like, "You are the way you are because of the way your parents were." While obviously true, such a statement is of no help to the person who wishes to be free of his parents' negative influence. The negative emotional autobiography provides not only the specifics of the individual negative traits but goes beyond that to show, in the client's own words, the scenes from his childhood in which he saw, heard, and felt mother or father expressing that trait with him. It is the clearest possible demonstration of the negative love syndrome in action, and it never fails to yield genuine understanding of the client's own life problems.

If the client resists the work, for example, by putting down the teacher while attempting to prove himself right, it is a simple matter to consult the negative trait list of mother or father and find the traits of "putting others down," "invalidated new ideas," and "had to be right all the time." Whenever examples like this come up, the client's awareness is directed to the negative trait list so that he fully understands the origin and meaning of his negative response: negative love to mother and father.

Everyone in the Process suffers from the disease of negative love, but each is afflicted in his own way. These differences and similarities are apparent in the three sets of notes that follow. As you experience these three people working through their negative love patterns in preparation for the later stages of the Process work, you will undoubtedly gain insights into yourself. While these may prove helpful to you, by themselves they cannot resolve the negative love syndrome. Only the fully emotional, gut-level experience of the Process, under the direction of a qualified teacher, can achieve the results shown here. Although not a do-it-yourself volume, the remainder of this book will be something like watching a good friend finding his positive essence. Carefully observing the procedure will increase your knowledge of the problem and its solution. It can also help you on your way, which is all anyone can expect from a book of this nature.

NANCY, THE HOSTILE

She was a tall, slender woman of 27. Her otherwise attractive appearance was marred by her slumped carriage and sullen expression. Alone with two small children after two broken marriages, she was aware that she had chosen unstable men who shared her inability to sustain an intimate relationship. Her work as a secretary left her frustrated and bored, but she could not decide what to do to change her life. She felt powerless to break free of her negative patterns despite her repeated efforts, and encouragement from her few friends.

The following excerpts from Nancy's negative emotional autobiography with mother show how her mother taught her to be both hostile and emotionally unexpressive. (Her father's role in her emotional problems is described later.) The autobiography ends with her puberty.

Nancy wrote:

> When I was born, my mother expected that I'd make up for all the disappointment and unhappiness in her life. Father was away a lot and didn't pay much attention to her when he was home. She really hated men. She thought they'd made things so hard for her. She figured my brothers belonged to my father, but that I didn't. She kept me away from him right from the beginning. She never really forgave either of my brothers for the hard time she had giving birth to them. She kept telling them what a good baby I was. Of course, they didn't like that, and they didn't like me much, either. All I wanted was to be loved and nourished, not to be used in her battles!
>
> We moved to another town when I was about three, and my mother told me we were only going to be there for a little while until my father would join us, so I kept waiting and looking for him, but he didn't come. I got madder and madder at her. She never wanted me to have a daddy. She took us away. Soon she started working in a restaurant downstairs from our apartment. My brothers went off by themselves most of the time, so I was alone with no one to take care of me. I was furious at her for taking me away from Daddy and then for leaving herself, but I was afraid to let her know. She'd get angry at me then and leave me even more.

I played with one little boy who was a year younger than me. Sometimes he was mean and tore my comic books. When I went running to tell my mother, she said I was a big girl and shouldn't complain, and she laughed about how cute he was. And I felt mean and ugly toward her, and that scared me even worse, so I tried to stop feeling anything at all.

When I was about six, we moved back together with my father for about six months. My mother was often in tears and angry, and they fought a lot. Once I heard her scream at him, "God will strike you dead for what you have done!" I was terrified and kept expecting a lightning bolt to hit us. My brothers stayed away from the house as much as they could, but I was too young to go anyplace, so I just hung around, feeling terrible, not understanding their fights and bitterness. We were all miserable, and she had brought us there. She made me behave politely to him while making it clear he was a bad man doing a terrible thing. I learned later he left us to live with another woman, but she didn't tell me anything at all. All I knew from her was that my daddy hated us.

Soon we moved again, away from my father, to a house in the country. We were three miles from the nearest town. Our one friend, who came occasionally with a car and goodies, was the relative who owned the house, an old man we called Uncle Teddy. I loved the attention I got from him. But I dreaded the way he touched me. Once I gathered up my courage and mumbled to my mother that Uncle Teddy was putting his hands inside my panties. She got hysterical, which made me terribly frightened. I felt as if I had done something shameful. She ordered me to tell her if he did it again. The next time he came over, she asked me if it had happened again. I lied, saying it had not, because I was so afraid of getting her all upset again. I felt angry and resentful that she hadn't protected me and scared because I couldn't depend on her.

Once a neighbor offered me 50 cents to drown three baby kittens. I'd watched my mother chop the heads off chickens, and my brothers shot game. It seemed like an OK way to make some money. My mother shamed me when she heard about it, making me feel as if I was inhuman and wicked. I felt confused and resentful, and terribly ashamed and bad. There was no way of knowing in advance what would draw all that emotionalism on my head. *Anything* I did was likely to turn out to be a bad thing. I became afraid to act.

About that time I became repelled at her body. She was somehow flabby, her underwear was ugly, and she was often sweaty, with a body odor I hated. When she tried to hold me, I stiffened. I didn't pull away because then she'd have asked me why, and I wouldn't have dared to tell her the truth. So I tried to control the pulling away and forced myself to pretend to hug back.

She believed it necessary to empty one's plate and forced me to eat food that sickened me. Creamed spinach was the worst. She'd give me a big portion, and then she'd eat a few tablespoons from my plate so that I wouldn't have so much of it to eat. I knew that she wanted me to appreciate her taking some away, but she'd put it there in the first place. That confused me because I felt angry and terribly relieved at the same time.

When I was 9, we moved to a town in Connecticut. My mother took us to a horror movie. It literally terrified me, and I hid under the seats, peeping out from between them. She was angry at me for "acting up." At the end of the show I pleaded with her to see it through again. Somehow I knew that if I could see it knowing how it ended, it would take some of the poison of terror away. As usual, she treated my serious request with contempt, sneering at me for having been so frightened, not understanding what I was asking for. All night long I would reach over and feel her fingernails to see if she were growing claws like the beast in the movie. I had to get up to pee repeatedly, and my pajamas were wet with the cold sweat of fear. Here she was, my own mother, and instead of being a haven of security, I imagined that she might turn into the savage, murderous beast!

When I was 12, I was elected editor of the class newspaper. This was special because it was very unusual for me to get positive notice from the other kids. When I told her they called me the "gossip columnist" of the class she looked disgusted and said she wouldn't want me to be that kind of person. I felt angry and resentful but as always said nothing to her. Again she had destroyed my smallest pleasure in relating to other children.

It was during this time, too, that she left a pamphlet on menstruation out where I would see it but could not bring herself to mention the subject to me. Again I felt a flash of resentment. I wanted her to talk to me about sex, to make it less strange and frightening, but she couldn't handle that, either.

My first menstrual period had no meaning for me. I went through it as I had learned to go through anything unpleasant—by turning off my connections with myself and simply watching as if it were happening to someone else.

Nancy's first menstrual period marks the onset of her puberty and the end of her negative love programming. She received a lengthy, paragraph-by-paragraph response to this Negative Emotional Autobiography on tape cassette. The hostility she had learned became overt during her teen-age years and was obvious in her sullenness and difficulty in relationships as an adult. At this point in the Process it was necessary for her to feel the hostility fully and direct it to her mother. After each paragraph I would comment indignantly. "So mother's already teaching you men are no good. Look at the relationships with men you had to break up in order to obey that negative trait. Two husbands already, and you are only 27!" I pointed out how her mother had created and encouraged the sibling rivalry that had robbed her of her brothers' love. I asked her what had happened to *them* with such a bitch mother, and her knowledge of their devastated adult lives (I knew they had to be) added fuel to her rage.

I supported her perceptions of how she had been taught to ignore and smother her own emotional responses, of how hard she had tried to learn to be a "good girl" to win the love of this unloving woman. I refused to let her blame her father at this point (his turn would come), but kept her focused on her mother's responsibility in driving him away and creating a miserable home life. I hammered at her with how undependable her mother's so-called love was, how she was on a seesaw and never knew where she stood. Her mother was only concerned with her own feelings, scaring the young Nancy with her own hysteria while neglecting her responsibility to comfort and support the girl when the old man (Uncle Teddy) sexually molested her.

Again and again I castigated her mother and drew Nancy's attention to what she was beginning to see: how the negative traits of her mother—angry, putting men down, unloving, uncaring, feeling superior, nonsupportive, unwilling to face reality, on and on through the 276 she had listed—had actually become her own by adoption through negative love. This helped her see herself more clearly and added fuel to her anger.

When she described her reaction to the horror movie incident, I assured her she was correct in seeing her mother as a murderous beast who might turn and claw her. In the bitch session her turn came to avenge herself against this woman who had all but destroyed her.

Simply bitching at mother, however, is not sufficient. Nancy's anger had to be directed at the particular behaviors and attitudes of mother that she adopted into her own personality. To help her see this, she was asked to review her list of mother's negative traits and decide for each if she adopted it out of negative love to mother or rebelled against it, throwing herself into conflict. We used a potent mind revelation to eliminate defensiveness. She really saw, with a shock, that she was her mother the bitch all over again. While the recognition is painful, it serves the vital purpose of further priming the pump of anger for the bitch session that follows. Nancy had little trouble with this since she was more than ready to let her mother have it. It was her declaration of independence from mother's negative traits.

Here is Nancy's description of her supervised bitch session:

> From my first words it was as if something took over inside me. I saw my mother—immobilized by my guide in my sanctuary—trying to control me with her eyes, looking enraged and warningly at me. And I flashed on the times that people have said to me that I had just such a black look. She herself had accused me of that. At that moment I started feeling real anger. I called her a "fucking hysterical bitch" and hit the pillow as hard as I could with the bat. My voice startled me—it was almost a scream. I kept yelling, "You stupid, stupid bitch!" and hitting with the bat. I kept

coming back to, "Do you know what you did to me, you stupid bitch?"

I was saying things to her I had never been able to say before—how she had, quite literally, destroyed my brothers, how she had warped my whole feelings about men and about myself, how I had to spend my whole life trying not to be like her—trying to tear her out of myself.

At one point I felt like she was looming over me, blotting out the whole world with her image, and I wanted to beat her down to normal size. (I kept hitting with the bat all this time with all my strength. Bob thrust some Kleenex into my hand, and I realized that my eyes and nose were streaming.) I kept yelling at her, 'You're just a normal-sized woman! You're not all that big!' I could literally see that huge image shrinking, and I kept beating at it.

Several times I felt exhausted and waited to see if I were finished, and then some new accusation would start boiling up inside. Then I'd go back to hitting and screaming, "You stupid bitch!" I accused her of blinding herself with rage, of being totally self-involved, hating me, driving my father away, not really loving anyone, feeling superior to other people, and at the same time being a fucking servant to them. Each time I spat out an indictment I immediately saw myself doing the same rotten thing she did and I got a spurt of renewed rage.

Afterwards I felt totally exhausted. It took five minutes to straighten my knees. I never noticed the pain while I was bitching at her and beating the pillows. I felt quieter inside and softer and relieved that the blocks were broken through. I felt more of a flow of life inside me.

After the session I felt that mother had been reduced to a normal-sized woman. Her neuroticism, her hysterical rages, her suffering, had always been larger than life. I began to see her as just a person (perhaps see myself as just a person), her tragedies no longer great, overwhelming disasters, her rages no longer to be feared like cataclysms. I felt as if some invisible mold that was holding me into a certain shape, "Don't be open, don't be like other people, be aloof, remember, you're better than all that (all of them)" had been shattered.

Nancy did more bitch sessions at home and in the woods until her fury was finally spent. She felt both exhausted and cleansed, for she had had an emotional purging that reached into the center of her being. She felt totally separate from her mother, no longer needing or wanting anything to do with her. She was now ready to take the next step, in the Defense section, of coming to understanding mother without condemnation.

CHRIS, THE ZOMBIE

As a psychologist with years of experience in various therapies, Chris had a clear intellectual understanding of his problems. Yet at age 46 his usually immobile features and the stiffness of his body indicated his "progress" had been mainly in the intellectual realm. He understood his inner deadness, the aridity of his relationships, and his occasional severe depressions but was unable to use his understanding of psychology to integrate his negative emotional self. He wrote:

> I was born in the middle of the night to a mother who wanted me to fulfill her role as mother and wife. Duty always came first, and she would put herself or her feelings down if they didn't fit her preconceptions. Being duty bound, she did everything by the book. She fed me by the clock because the book said to. I was forced to her mold quite early and conformed readily. My feelings and needs were hardly even existent unless the pediatrician or baby book said so.
>
> I recall being dropped in a bathinette during infancy. My mother let my head fall under water while I gasped and choked on the water, scared and hurt. Lesson number 1: I may be dependent for my existence on Mom, but I sure can't always trust her.
>
> From very early Mother was very busy with clubs, charities, and travel. I remember at the age of two, sister Anne (age 5) and I were dumped with a woman for weeks—I don't know how many. I do remember not wanting her to leave, being taken to the backyard where there were toys, swings, etc., while she talked with the lady. When I came back inside, she had gone. Both Anne and I got the flu and were sick during that stay. I was so confused when she

returned I'm not sure I was even glad to see her. Lesson number 1 reinforced, as well as number 2: I'm essentially powerless, and number 3: My feelings are not important.

Mother had many, many sayings about how to act, to feel, etc. One I remember well seemed to begin about age 3. If I complained about something I got, "Be happy if you can, cheerful if you must, and pleasant if it *kills you.*" I cursed her many times under my breath for that one. Be phony, be perfect, show a good front to the world, don't inconvenience anyone else by my feelings, they don't count.

Whenever I would get into some situations where I was learning something new or trying something that didn't come off, she had a favorite expression for putting me down, spitefully bruising my self-esteem: "Well, I won't say I told you so." I remember this from age 4 on, and at least once I said, "I wish you wouldn't say, 'I told you so.' You tell me not to be nasty like that." She jumped all over me, denying that she was being nasty. Double talking was OK if you had the power to make your denial stick. Lesson: Don't talk back or try to reason with the unreasonable, especially mother.

Probably the most damaging and frustrating thing she did to me over many years was to directly deny that my experience was what I said it was. My statement might be something as personal and private as, "I don't like asparagus." She would then answer, "Of course you do, you know you do." Message: My feelings were either not important, or I didn't really have the experiences I thought I had. Whenever she used to do this, I would go into instant internal rage with an urge to shout, throw things, swear, although I don't ever remember acting on this.

She used to rub my back to put me to sleep as late as 10 years old, but it was usually after I asked her to. She would then say, "What's the matter, dear, aren't you feeling well?" Lesson: It's not OK to want to touch/love except when something is wrong.

Her nagging was the most common greeting when we would meet in the same room. "When are you going to . . ." meaning, "If I don't remind you, you aren't competent to do it." This was applied to doctor's appointments, paper route, homework, writing Christmas thank yous, etc.

My response was almost always swallowed, suppressed anger and procrastination on those things.

I came home once after being hit on the head (it later turned out to be a concussion), while a Cub Scout meeting was in progress. I told mother I wasn't feeling well and was going to lie down. She said that was fine and continued her duties as den mother. (I wanted her to dismiss the meeting and attend to me. "Hey! I'm your son—hurt, angry, rejected.")

I wish I could have seen her get really mad at least once. She often showed displeasure to me—tight lips, refusal to talk about something, but I have no recollection of her speaking ill of anyone until long after my puberty. This includes the Axis during the war. I have a vague recollection of asking her and being told, "It's not nice to think bad thoughts about other people."

Mother stayed out of any discussion of sex. I never thought much of Mother regarding sex and puritanism, but I do remember how stuffy and scared of talking about it she was. Occasionally Dad would tell an off-color joke about sex. Mother never seemed to laugh. I recall realizing something was wrong. I thought some of his jokes funny, but Mother didn't approve, so I couldn't laugh. She would say it was all right but stiffen and otherwise show she didn't approve.

Note the contrast between Chris's emotional autobiography and Nancy's. Unlike her, he coats much of his resentment with a vacillating, saccharine-sweet tone. In the feedback his games and evasions were called so that he began to see mother, and his feelings toward her, as they really were, not as mother manipulated him into seeing them. At each opportunity during the Process I indignantly goaded and taunted him while unmercifully castigating his mother in order to arouse his deadened ire and resentment. Since Zombies are often so resistant to bitching at Mother, I use the tool of negative transference to arouse their anger toward me first, and when it is powerful enough, and they are ready to explode, I redirect the anger from me to the bitch mother. Chris's bitch session shows how effective this technique is.

"From your babyhood, Chris," I told him, "mother is telling you how to act and feel. Be pleasant if it kills you? She killed you, all right. She split you in two. You now have a negative emotional child at war with your adult intellect. You're a neurotic wreck. Your lifelong therapies have failed you. For this you can thank your bitch mother. You can't love yourself, your wife, your children, or anyone else in your life. Your mother killed you, all right. She is a bitch! You've become a Zombie just like her."

In answer to his comments about his mother's sexual attitudes I told him, "If a woman expects a son to become a sexually fulfilled man, he must have no fear of women. Your model of women is your mother. If your mother doesn't speak of sex, then women must, in some way, be deficient in sex. You learned the message: Women, mothers, aren't interested in sex, they don't talk about sex with their children. All of this, Chris, comes from just one sentence you wrote, 'Mother stayed out of any discussion of sex.' That one line tells it all. Her acts of omission were as negative as her sins of commission."

I also asked Chris to tell me how much he trusted his wife. Was his wife a reflection of mother, who had him on a seesaw of love, sometimes up, sometimes down? Here's his answer:

"No, I do not trust my wife very much with my feelings and have been much afraid of her. I have trusted her from time to time and often been disappointed. I do trust several other women. My closest friends are women, in terms of trust, but not in terms of time spent with them."

Every woman in a close relationship represents mama in some way. A wife, especially to a man who isn't emotionally mature, is always a mother figure. The same applies to women in their relations with men. The husband is a father figure.

Because of his negative love pattern with his mother, Chris couldn't possibly trust his wife. His closest friends are women, he says, although he doesn't see them often. He learned it was OK to trust women he sees rarely since they couldn't really hurt him. If he doesn't spend much time with them, he will have no opportunity to learn to distrust them, which is his negative pattern created by his mother.

After the feedback Chris then wrote:

Bob, as I worked with "negative Mother," it felt at first like a great distortion, almost like lying, to talk of the negatives without balancing them with the positives. Many of the negatives were present, true, but only part of the time. As I have gone over and over the material, the negative is there. I do feel anger, frustration, and resentment at Mother. I have to keep redirecting it, as now I tend to turn it on myself and excuse her, which is my game, but *now* I see it.

Looking at the list (of Mother's negative traits, moods, and admonitions), I went from numbness to a sense of, "I've known that before"—but in the past, whenever I looked, I had to look away, feeling disgust and only a flash of anger at her. (I'm not allowed to be angry.) This was followed in previous glimpses by denial, rationalization, or some other defense where I told myself either I wasn't really living that trait, or it was OK to be that way. (After all, Mother is like that.)

This time I looked and saw myself showing many of these negative traits with Bob. Underneath some stirring of feelings of self-disgust, anger at Mother, curses at the world for being like it is, and hanging on to the promise of a way out of this emotional swamp. Curious revelation: *I am my mother! Gulp! Wow!*

The insight Chris reached after his negative emotional autobiography is the goal toward which much of the preceding work was aimed. Chris had to see how his own most troubling problems, particularly the inability to love himself and others, came directly from the stultifying manipulations and deceits of his mother. All of what went before was done specifically to enable him to see *and feel* the impact of *"I am my mother."* After that the only thing to do is give him room and protection while he opened the flood gates of his blocked emotions and declared his independence from mother.

The day after his supervised bitch session he wrote out another one.

"Mother" (I put that in quotes because the title is false, unearned, and the most hated of all epithets), I want you to suffer my hate. You deserve me as you've made me—

afraid of people, indecisive, negative attention getter. Fuck you! I hate the You in Me. You couldn't recognize real feelings, and you taught me to ignore them. You fucked me over royally. I throw up your teaching! I want you to drown in my vomitus. Three times down and *no* help—I turn my back on you and abandon you as you abandoned me.

My throat hurts, I can hardly talk, yet I want to shout, Fuck you, Mother! You couldn't sing—so I can't sing. That alone you should die for. How can any man live without singing his feelings? Croak yourself. Suffer in silence, you martyr. You had no right to hurt me this way. You fucking bitch, you've got me crying again—but now I'm going to cry for myself—never again for you and not even because of you. I won't let you stop me from feeling ever again. I'm going to feel my hatred, my anger for you. If I have to throw up and throw up, I'll do so gladly to get rid of you and your bilious, vile sourness in me. Damn you! Damn you! Damn you! I don't need injections of hate and anger. All I need is to think of you.

Where were you when I needed you? I cried in my pillow but, you bitch, you couldn't hear 'cause you taught me to be self-sufficient. Goddamn liar! There's another of your games I took over—self-pity. I don't want your games, I don't need your games, *I won't continue to play them.* Hear me, Mother! I'm telling you now, I hate you, I hate your hypocrisy, I hate your phony love, your mechanical, sentimental shit. I hate your fault-finding, critical, perfect fucking self right down to your rotten selfish leave-me-alone center. Take your whole nice, moral, "loving," indirect head and choke on your own shit!

You never gave me a straight message in your life. No! Now I'm so Goddamn overresponsible I can't enjoy myself. You've made me so compulsive I feel guilty all the time unless I've read everything, written everything, and done all my duties. You fucking compulsive whore! (I threw up here, breathed, and continued.)

Oh, I'm like you, all right! I'm like you right down to my fucking toes: pacifying, afraid of everything, smooth it over before it even gets going. You fucked me up thoroughly. You shut off conflict, shut off confronting—just lie down and get walked on 'cause that's the way it's supposed to be.

That's not the way it's supposed to be! You lied to me about everything. You lied about love, you lied about caring, you lied about people. You bullied and double messaged me into a shitty little scared, wishy-washy half man, half thing like you.

(After vomiting again, fatigued, shaking, with upset stomach and cramped muscles, I rested a few minutes. Then I closed my eyes and took a mind revelation to my sanctuary where I looked a long time at my mother tied to a stake. She was a collapsed, bleeding blob. I told my guide to throw the thing out and not let it back in unless I said to. He quickly grabbed her, threw her bodily and roughly into the tunnel, and slammed the door.)

I'm still shaking, my whole body is tingling with a flow of energy up and down and across the entire surface of my being. I feel relieved and think I've passed some sort of step. Maybe I'll have to do it again, but it won't be the same. I really feel like after a race or exhausting swim. I'm at the other side resting on the beach.

As I write this, I'm so tired and yet excited that I'm not sure what I'm feeling. My mouth tastes as if I were recovering from a hangover.

P.S. (the next day): Last night I woke up at 3 A.M. with the most glorious, fantastic energy *vibrating* throughout my whole body. I know some doors are opening to me as I get ready for them.

The doors that were opening for Chris, like those for Nancy, lead away from the negativity he adopted from mother.

LAURA, THE BAYGULL

Nothing is as it appears to be. Laura was a small, pretty brunette who made her living selling real estate. She had a cheerful demeanor and a ready smile. Though unmarried at 35, she maintained that her life was generally satisfactory. After some probing, however, she admitted having had periods of depression and suicidal thoughts since her teen years. She also acknowledged her inability to feel comfortable in a close relationship with a man. She was aware of her considerable resentment toward her father, while believing she had been close with her mother. She saw her mother as nearly above criticism and found it hard to believe she had any angry feelings toward her. The development of her psychic abilities in the Process permitted her to go back before her birth and re-experience all of what had really happened to her. Once she did, she soon learned the truth about her mother.

> When I am three months in the womb and first begin to sense things around me, I recognize that my mother is very anxious. She is pregnant with me and doesn't want to be. My father is insisting on an abortion. My mother is hurt and confused. She always submits to her husband, is dutiful, and absolutely compliant. However, he has at last asked for too much. She cannot bring herself to have an abortion. The operation is illegal, dangerous, costly, and totally unacceptable to her puritanical mind. Her guilt would be too keen. Besides, suppose she were found out? What would people think of a married woman who did such an unspeakable thing? Because of this I am saved.
>
> A month after she had expected me, I am finally born. It is midnight. I feel frightened by what is happening to me. I feel muscular contractions forcing me from my secret hiding place. Cold metal forceps grasp my head. I come screaming, cold, frightened, into the blinding lights and the cool, impersonal hands of the doctor, who promptly passes me to the nurse. My mother moans in her drugged state. She is barely aware of me. She focuses on her pain rather than on me. I want immediately to be reassured, fondled, breast fed, loved. Instead, I am taken to a nursery full of crying babies and left alone.
>
> With resignation, the way she sighs and submits to unpleasant things, my mother accepts my existence and is glad I am a girl. Little girls are cute, you can dress them in sweet dresses. Mother will have a little playmate, since she is a little girl emotionally herself. She picks the name Laura Rose for me.
>
> I am 2. My Mommy always keeps my hair curled, and I wear pink playsuits with frilly edges. But she treats me like a doll, not a living being. Even though she makes such a big deal about my being a little girl, she is tense about the idea

of my being female. She is careful not to let me see my Daddy naked. I take baths with my mother until one day I notice she has brown tits. From then on she bathes me by myself. I learn there is something wrong with having a body. It is to be covered up and ignored.

When I am 3, I hear the lady next door playing the piano. It is the most beautiful sound I have ever heard. I want more than anything else to make that heavenly music. Whenever I get a chance, I strike the keys on the lady's piano. I discover that my aunt has one, too. I can't wait to go to my aunt's house. When I get there, my mother says, "Stop that noise, silly. Go off and play." I ask for a piano, but she doesn't take me seriously. At Christmas time I ask Santa Claus for a piano. My mother laughs at me and tells Santa, "You remember, Santa, how small our house is." Eventually, almost every child on the block has a piano except me. As much as I want one, my mother does not go to bat for me to see that I get one. I learn very early not to ask for those things I want most, as I know for sure that once people know what I want they will know what to take away.

She is almost always even-tempered. No matter what happens, "Everything is fine," she says. My father throws a temper tantrum, and she pretends it didn't happen. He says the same thing over and over again, and she never stops him. The weather is always sunny for my mother, and her placid smile never seems to vary. If something really unpleasant happens, she just closes her lips tight and will not talk about it. If I do something she doesn't like, she just ignores it and pretends it never happened.

One day we are in the bedroom, and my father begins to tickle my mother. She twists away from him and makes a face. He keeps right on. Mother says, "Stop. You're hurting me." My Daddy throws her on the bed. She says, "Not in front of Laura." I think Daddy is hurting her, so I pick up a comb from the dresser and throw it between them. Now both of them are mad at me for interfering. Mother doesn't like either one of us. I feel that she is unfair, refusing to understand why I threw the comb. Mother is always uncomfortable if Daddy touches her while I am around. I learn it is not nice to let a man touch you.

When I am 8 my aunt sends a box of books from where she is living in New York. Among the books is one about sex and babies for children. I ask about the book, but my mother seems reluctant to let me read it. I notice where she puts it and take it out and read it. I learn that babies grow inside their mothers, although I still don't understand how they get there. One day I am sitting on the back porch with a neighbor boy while our mothers talk across the fence. I tell Donnie he was very small when he lived inside his mother. At once my mother whisks me away. My mother tells me, "I don't ever want to hear you talking about such a thing again." I feel that I have done a terrible thing and wonder whether I will be allowed to play with Donnie again. I am careful to avoid the subject of sex from then on. I learn that it is a bad thing to have a baby. Being female (or male) must also be a bad thing.

One day I give away my stuffed toys to the woman next door, who runs a day nursery. My mother cries. I feel that I must be hardhearted and cruel, so I give in to my mother's wishes and get the toys back.

During my grade school days, from time to time my mother has me come down on the bus from school and meet her at the depot. We go to the dime store for lunch, and sometimes we go to a movie. My mother makes me promise not to tell Daddy that we did these things. I can't imagine why not. I am uncomfortable about slipping around to do something fun and then not telling Daddy. Also, I don't like thinking that doing something fun has to be a secret and something you do when men are not around.

I learn that women are helpless. They have almost no money from their stingy husbands except grocery money, and they have to dip into this in order to have a little innocent fun. Men are ogres, and women are sweet, innocent victims!

When I am 12, my folks buy me an accordion for Christmas. I have wanted a piano for nine years, but I get an accordion instead. My mother likes accordion music, "oldie but goodie" tunes like "Blackbird, Bye-Bye." *She* likes the accordion. I do not. She assumes I will like the same tunes she likes. I want to learn classical music. I feel angry and resentful. I want to be a musician, not a player of pop music at afternoon teas. My mother thinks this is cute. I resent her forcing her musical taste on me.

We make fudge and popcorn every Sunday one winter. A whole tray of candy and a big bowl of popcorn. Overeating, a forbidden pleasure. "We'll get fat," she says. I still feel guilty whenever I eat chocolate candy.

When I am 13 I begin to menstruate. I think perhaps I am incontinent, like my aging grandmother. With tight lips, my mother shows me how to use a Kotex and belt and tells me never to get blood on my outside clothes. I haven't any idea what this nuisance of menstruation is all about. But I know better than to ask. My mother will never speak, except by indirection, of sex.

My mother never discusses money with me. It is as taboo as sex. Whatever she knows about that, she passes none of it on to me, just as she never discusses her relatives. She is an ostrich; I learned to be one, too.

The clarity and detail with which Laura was able to go back into her childhood allowed her to re-experience and rediscover her true feelings toward her mother. To bring her anger to fever pitch I goaded her again and again with the effects of her mother's treatment of her; how her mother had not wanted her and refused the abortion only out of self-concern for what the neighbors would think of her and the difficulties involved; how her mother had never taken her seriously as a being with needs and rights of her own; had cheated her out of her early love of music. I supported her perception of how her mother's attitudes toward her father and sex had shaped her own and robbed her of the ability to love a man.

I pointed out how her mother's refusal to let her grow up had created her current difficulty in functioning as an adult woman. I pushed her particularly hard on how her mother had taught her to fix that same placid smile on her face, which created the outward Baygull look that masked her smoldering hostility. With my response to each paragraph of her work, the façade of "always looking on the bright side," another destructive trait of mother's, began to crumble. As she examined her list of mother's 315(!) negative traits and their debilitating effect on her, she had no difficulty realizing how she had adopted mother's traits out of negative love and become mother all over again. Stripped of mother's false sweetness, she was primed and ready to give it all back to her.

Her bitch session follows:

> I have this scared feeling. I can't do this. It's frightening to release this much. I don't think I can do it. Nothing will come out but a squeak. Then I took the preparatory mind revelation and I start.
>
> You fucking bitch, listen to me. I said *Listen to me!* Don't put your hands over your Goddamned ears. *Listen!* You whore, you witch! I hate you for every fucking lie you taught me; for every cold, empty, ugly way you made me feel about myself. I'm tired of being your puppet, your doll, your goody-goody on the outside and as full of shit as you are on the inside. You bore me. You're boring. You're shallow, insincere, and boring. I puke you up! I'm sick of not loving myself, you bitch, and feeling it was wrong to love myself because you didn't love me. You never knew who I was. All you wanted was a baby doll to dandle on your lap when company came. You didn't care about me. Well, Goddamn it, *I'm me! I'm over here! See me!* You bitch, you always put your hands over your eyes when you didn't want to see something bad. *Look at me!*
>
> You bitch, you never wanted to see me, did you? I begged you for a piano, but *you* didn't want one, so you couldn't imagine why I would want one. Because I'm me, Goddamn it, not you. *I'm not you! I don't want to be like you. I'm me!* I don't want to spend my life alone, an old maid, gray, colorless, and boring. I don't want to obey your admonition—don't fuck, don't enjoy, don't love, don't, don't, don't! I want to be, to do. I want positive things in my life, not the emptiness of things and people you gave me. I don't want to be invisible anymore—and I won't be! *I don't want to be an ostrich like you!* I want to see myself as I am—an ugly bitch by adoption. But I won't be a bitch like you anymore, so take back your shit, you no-mother mother! *Go to hell, Mommy!* I'm sick of your compulsions, your hangups, your fear of living and loving. I'm sick of the garbage you put in my brain, the shit you put in my heart, the vomit you stuffed in my gut. I won't have your poison in my system anymore!

I'm not afraid of you anymore, Mommy. All my life I've been afraid of you. "Don't do this. Don't do that. Don't enjoy that. Be good." So afraid of Mommy. She might take her love away if I don't dance like her puppet. *Bullshit!* You never loved me, anyway. I've stunted and denied my life for you, and *you didn't even care, you bitch!*

I have a word for you, Mother. The word for you is *No!* You want me to say, "Yes, Mommy, yes. I'll be your baby. Yes, I'll eat your garbage. Yes, I'll love you. Yes, I'll be a nothing for you." Well, I don't say 'Yes' anymore, Mommy. I say *No!! No, No, No, No, No, No,* from now on *No!* Never again will I eat your shit. Go to hell, Mommy. From now on I'm me!

Afterward I am completely dazed. I don't know exactly where I have been. I almost lost consciousness of the others. Mostly I am aware of my own feelings, my vigorous movement with the pillow (I have never beaten anything so hard), of the cries and screams that well up from deep inside, my sense of loss and outrage, and pain, and anger. I expected to cry, but I didn't. I cried *out.* When I open my eyes I feel weak, and the room looks unreal to me, and the people in it. It is like coming to after an operation—disorientation about time and place. My body is tired. I feel lightheaded and light inside. An amazing thing happened this morning when I woke up. I had only six hours of sleep and usually feel kind of rocky after that, but instead I feel good—rested, light. I'm not sure what has happened to me. I hope it is the beginning of a new way to be, a new freedom from my mother.

After Mother's bitch session most people feel remarkably similar: a mixture of exhaustion, cleanliness, and relief. While they are purged of their anger toward mother, (and no one is allowed to continue in the Process until they are), they are not finished with her. For the moment they are instructed to leave mother's negative crud piled in a corner of the sanctuary. Later, father's negativity will be added to the compost heap, to be used for recycling in the final session.

How are you feeling about your mother now?

7. "Everyone Is Guilty and No One Is to Blame"

Mother. *Mutter. Mere. Madre.* In any language or culture the word calls forth powerful images. Close your eyes for a moment, see and think of all you associate with the word "mother." (Although after the previous chapter you may see only negative images of mother, try to do the exercise anyway.)

After taking some time to free associate on "mother," what have you come up with? A long list of motherly attributes? Some physical characteristics of mothers, perhaps? Possibly you saw some childhood scenes of you and mother together.

If you are like most people, you associate "mother" with an adult woman. We usually picture mothers as grown and mature, at least physically. While our normal visualization of mother is accurate, seeing her only as an adult blinds us to a crucial truth: Mother was a child once herself. While everyone "knows" their mother was once a child, the full meaning of this fact is not appreciated by most of us. We tend to feel and think about mother as the grown woman we looked up to: larger, stronger, older, more knowing and supposedly more loving than we were. That first emotional impression of mother's infallibility is a lasting one. (It is also a chief cause of negative love patterns. If mother knows what is right, and we don't, then doing things her [negative] way will appear natural and proper to the child.) Our later understanding that mother was not an ideal model to follow has less impact on us since it is usually no more than an intellectual experience. The unfortunate result of this misperception is that we cannot normally appreciate in a deep emotional way how much like our own is the negative love tragedy mother suffered as a child. The next stage in the removal of the negative love pattern is the Defense of Mother, which serves to remedy this critical deficiency in the emotional bond with her.

A dramatic turning point takes place after mother's Prosecution. The total personal absorption, physical, emotional, intellectual, and spiritual, in the bitching leaves people exhausted but exhilarated, like an athlete after a hard-won victory. Remember what it was like the last time you went all out physically in a game or at work. That thrilling mixture of strength, tiredness, relaxation, and most of all, aliveness and victory, is exactly what you feel after the exertions of bitching at mother over the course of a week.

This state of relaxed openness makes possible the abrupt and thorough shift from the negativity of mother's prosecution to the positivity of her defense. It also clears the way for you to see and experience mother beyond the adult she was to the child she had been long before you knew her. Until you make mother's childhood a part of yourself in more than an intellectual way, any pretense of understanding her is false and premature. To simply say, "Oh, yes, I know she had it tough as a kid," without experiencing it fully and deeply is just another intellectual game, with no lasting positive effect. It is essential to experience her childhood in order to attain a real gut-level understanding of this woman who was your mother.

The truth of the negative love syndrome is that *everyone is guilty and no one is to blame.* Whether aware of it now or not, we carry the anger toward mother inside us all our lives (unless we do something to free ourselves of it). We judged her guilty of unlovingness during our childhood and continued to blame her ever after. True, she is guilty of all the cold, unloving acts recalled in the negative emotional autobiography. *But she is not to blame.* Mother did what she did because of the parents she had. Your parents programmed you to be the way you are, and her parents programmed her to be the way she was.

During the Prosecution of Mother it is right and proper to bitch at her for the wrongs she did. Now, in the Defense of Mother, is the time to go beyond blaming to understanding.

There are five steps in learning to love. The first of the five steps in learning to love is to understand *without condemnation.* The second step is learning compassion, which the dictionary defines as "profound feeling for the misfortune of others and a desire to aid them" or "sorrow for another's plight or predicament accompanied by a strong desire to eliminate the pain or remove its cause." (The final three steps are taken in Closure, described in Chapter 12.)

When we look beneath the level of sentimental sympathy, it is possible to find real, gut-level, insightful understanding. Who was this woman, your mother? What was she all about? You may have thought you knew her well, but did you? What were mother's parents (your grandparents) really like? Forget the white-haired folks with bifocals you may remember fondly from your childhood. Consider instead the young parents they were in their twenties and thirties, with all their teeth and no wrinkles. What was it like for mother to have been the child of your grandparents? (All the rude questions we asked about your love life, sex life, childhood with mother, and so forth, are relevant to mother as well as to you.) Whatever it was like, her family experience made your mother the child she was, the woman and wife she became, and the mother you knew. You can use your natural sensory perception abilities to psychically see mother's childhood programming. Through this procedure you can hear her describe her childhood from her perspective. In the Prosecution stage everyone sees himself as the victim of mother the bitch. In the Defense stage we learn to see mother as the victim of *her* bitch mother and bastard father.

The metaphor of two sides of a coin helps make the point that prosecuting mother for her sins of omission and commission is one-sided. The other side of the coin is that if you are 30 years old and your mother is 60, she has endured the affliction of unloveability twice as many years as you have and she deserves twice as much compassion as you do. You can still avoid living out the remainder of your life doomed never to experience even one totally loving relationship, but your mother probably won't make it. If she is still alive, she will probably die with that lonely, hurt, frightened little girl still trapped inside her.

(Of course, it is never too late to learn to love. The oldest person to go through the Process so far is a 74-year-old woman who got a loving divorce from her long-dead parents and learned to love her children, and her grandchildren, for the first time.)

If your mother is already dead, how much more poignant is her love tragedy. After all those years of living in the wasteland of no real love, she never made it. She went to her grave unloved and unloving.

The explanation of mother's tragic lack of love in life is largely the same as yours: No one taught her to love during her formative childhood years. She could not teach you what she herself never learned. She received the disease of negative love from her mother and father just as you got it from your parents. They got it from their parents, who got it from their parents, who got it from *their* parents, and so on back in time and space like a contagious disease, all the way back to the first men and women. Think of negative love as the world's most common, most highly infectious disease.

By overthrowing the force of negative love, you can absolve yourself and mother of her karma for the negativities and unloveability she inflicted on her children. (In this regard, karma means not only paying for the debts you incurred in past lifetimes but also spiritual progression to overcome the negativities experienced here and now.) It is possible to clear mother's karma if you rid yourself of your negative love for her and progress nearer to the Godhead from which we all come. The worst of all the karmic debts we take upon ourselves in this lifetime is the perpetuation of negative love patterns. Replacing them with loving positivity is the way to spiritual progression and enlightenment.

While the chain of negative love reaches endlessly backward in time, it does not have to continue forward into the future. Yours can be the link that is broken, permanently ending the negative continuity. Once you understand what your parents did to you through negative love, you have a right to be deeply concerned about the damage you may be doing to your own children.

The psychic technology of mind revelations is used extensively in the Defense of Mother. In the first stage of the defense a dialogue takes place between the client's negative emotional child at age 13 (or whenever puberty occurred) and mother's negative emotional child at about the same age. The conversation between the two children, in which mother's child answers important questions about her childhood, produces an understanding of the emotional deprivation she experienced. What the child within mother describes to the client is often quite similar to his own trauma, making it possible for the two to empathize with each other. Note that the dialogue, like the remainder of the Defense of Mother, is not a fantasy or guided imagery. It is a mind revelation employing natural sensory perception abilities to receive and tune into the emotional experiences of mother's past. Strange as it may seem, this mind revelation always produces the necessary beneficial results. Everyone succeeds in doing it fully.

The next step after the dialogue is the monologue, in which mother's psychic Trinity, with the knowledge gleaned from the dialogue, dictates to the client her negative emotional autobiography with her own mother and father. She recounts her own childhood programming. It is usually shocking to discover that mother's childhood was similar in its loneliness, frustration, and lack of parental warmth and love. In the monologue she gives a year-by-year account of how she, like him, grew up with manipulation, deceit, and no consistent love. Mother learned her negativity the same way he did, from Mama and Papa.

The dialogue, followed by the monologue, prepares the way for the Trial-log, which integrates mother's defense. It is the log of a trial with three participants:

1. The client's negative emotional child at age 13
2. Mother's adult Trinity at the age when the client was 13
3. The client's spiritual self, who acts as judge-moderator

In the Trial-log the client's negative emotional child has its final opportunity to purge itself of any residual anger and resentment toward mother. It begins like a second bitch session. But this time mother, with her newly acquired knowledge of her childhood programming, uses her adult intellect to defend herself against the accusations. The client's vengeful child may want to continue to gripe and complain over the wrongs mother did, instead of developing his understanding with no condemnation. The client's spiritual self is present, however, to intervene and make sure his child does understand and is willing to experience deeply the other side of mother, the side that was crippled emotionally in her childhood and left powerless to do other than she did. The client's spiritual self influences him to cease blaming mother and replace the vengeance with compassionate understanding.

After this three-step mind revelation process it is possible to leave behind all negativity, hostility, bitching, and anger at mother while moving closer to learning to love her and yourself. The actual Defense of Mother is followed by still another mind revelation, Mother's Compassion Scene. In this procedure the client sees, and then emotionally experiences, mother's death as though it were happening now. He experiences it as real, whether she is still alive or already gone. Seeing mother going to her grave, actually being lowered into the ground with her unloved negative emotional child still trapped within her, evokes great sadness and grief over the senseless tragedy of her unfulfilled, loveless, emotionally barren life. The client cries bitter tears of sadness and compassion for her wasted life as an unloved woman, wife, and mother. When experienced with full emotionality, mother's funeral always calls forth compassionate sobbing and crying, since he sees her as she really was and is: alone, unloved, and now beyond help. His earlier angry shouting has turned to compassionate crying as he learns the emotional reality of their life together: Her tragedy duplicates and exceeds his own.

Reading about the experience of Mother's Defense is tame in comparison to living it as Laura, Nancy, and Chris did. Each of them lived through a powerful, unsettling, but ultimately life-restoring transformation in their Defense of Mother. To show the flavor of the work they did, excerpts from their notes are presented. The emotional impact of the three steps of the defense is cumulative, but the information itself is much the same. For the sake of brevity, therefore, only one segment from each defense is given: (1) Laura's dialogue with her mother's 13-year-old negative emotional child, (2) Chris's monologue, in which his mother dictates her negative emotional autobiography with her mother and father, and (3) Nancy's Trial-log of her negative emotional child, her mother's adult Trinity, and her (Nancy's) spiritual self as judge-moderator. Chris's description of Mother's Funeral Scene, which concludes the chapter, is typical of the experience of most clients.

LAURA'S DIALOGUE WITH MOTHER

In this discussion with her mother's child at puberty, Laura comes to see at first-hand the origin of mother's negative traits that have caused her so much suffering. Her mother, Alice, had been programmed by her parents to be unloving, a goody-goody, falsely cheerful, obsessed with appearances, and many other negative traits to which Laura responded with either adoption or rebellion. Within these excerpts of that dialogue, you will see how Laura came to understand the meaning of negative love patterns as they expressed themselves in her life, and how her mother was also a victim of this emotional affliction.

After a mind revelation to prepare her, the dialogue begins.

> My mother appears in the sanctuary, and my guide asks mother's intellect and mine to observe and learn but not to interfere. Now it is just my negative emotional child at puberty confronting my mother's emotional child at the same age.
>
> LAURA: Hello, little girl who grew up to be my mother. How was it with you and your parents?
>
> ALICE: Most of my childhood was unhappy. When I was just a little baby, my father died. (We were happier until then. Mother said he was always cheerful and smiling.) He had some kind of heart attack during the night, and my mother didn't know what to do for him. She didn't understand how sick he was, and in the morning he was dead. All her life after that she felt she had killed him, and she never got over it.
>
> LAURA: That must have been terrible!
>
> ALICE: It was very sad for all of us. My mother and my aunts and my big brother cried, and I cried, too. After that I never knew what it was to have a father. I always longed for a father. I would have liked to sit on my Daddy's lap and have him hold me the way I saw some of my friends' fathers do.
>
> LAURA: That does sound lonely.
>
> ALICE: My mother always was sad after my father died, though she pretended to feel all right in front of outsiders. I tried to comfort her as best I could, but I just felt helpless

because I couldn't. We were very poor, too. My mother didn't know how to support us, and she was always worried about food and clothing.

LAURA: So you were afraid and worried and feeling helpless when you were a little girl. And you were sad because your mother was sad, but that didn't make her feel any better.

ALICE: Sometimes I felt that my mother would have been better off if I hadn't been born. I felt guilty for being around, for being another mouth to feed.

LAURA: Didn't that make you feel resentful? Did you sometimes hate your mother for making you feel unwanted?

ALICE: I'm ashamed to admit that, but it's true. Sometimes I secretly hated my mother for making me feel so wretched. But then I tried even harder to *act* happy around her so that I'd make up for being angry at her. Most of all I resented the way she preferred my brother John to me. He was her first baby, and she loved him in a way she never loved me. She felt that I was just another ignorant female like her who didn't know how to save her husband's life or earn a living for her children. She really despised herself for being a woman, and so she despised me for being a woman, too.

LAURA: I'm beginning to see why you were so uncaring and cold to me. You never were treated with love yourself.

ALICE: Yes. I know I have seemed cold to you, and I have been. But I didn't know how to be warm and affectionate. I never learned that from my only parent. I never felt OK inside, or worthy or happy. I decided I wouldn't be sad like my mother. I'd be like my daddy had been. So I learned to smile all the time and pretend that everything was all right. It never felt right inside. But I thought if I didn't upset mother, maybe she would love me.

LAURA: I'm beginning to see where you got so much of your negativity. But how about being so manipulative? You tried to make me into a puppet.

ALICE: I had to learn how to manipulate people because there wasn't any other way of getting what I wanted. I knew nobody loved me enough to give me anything, so I had to get it some other way. My mother manipulated John and me with her cold silences, her sad looks, and her criticism. I decided never to do that, but I guess I ended up doing it, anyway. I wanted so many things I couldn't have when I was a little child. Even new, warm underwear would have been a treat. So I thought when I grew up and became a mother I would give my children lots of things, birthday parties, Christmas gifts, and pretty clothes, and then they would always love me.

LAURA: You learned how to act loving even if you didn't feel it.

ALICE: I did what I thought mommies ought to do: Kiss the baby and hold it when company came. I thought a clean, well-dressed baby was a loved baby. I became a Pollyanna, pretending that everything was all right because that was the way I thought I could get my mother to love me. I was a good little girl for my mother. I swept and washed dishes and sewed. I walked on tiptoes around her. I still am a very good girl even though I'm almost grown up now. I try to do whatever my mother wants, and in many ways I am just like her, but it doesn't help. It seems as if all my life she is saying to me, "I'll love you if you're good, or quiet, or helpful, or if you comfort me. Now go away."

After much more discussion, Laura was able to say,

> I understand your life now. I really can't condemn you. You just didn't have much choice. You were in as much pain as I have been.

During and after this dialogue Laura understood with no condemnation why her mother treated her as she did. She had no doubt she was talking with the child who grew up to become her mother. Mind revelations do not lie. She experienced the mind revelation as real and, like others who have done it, gleaned new information about her mother's childhood which she was able to verify with her parents or other relatives. The emotional essence of the dialogue is always true. Mother was negatively programmed by the grandparents and unwittingly passed it along to her children.

Once the facts of mother's negative love programming and

emotional anguish are clear, the second step is to put the scenes in chronological order. Mother's story, like the client's, must be reconstructed. Chris has already had his dialogue with his mother and understands the forces that shaped her. Now she puts in autobiographical form for him the story of her negative love training to become the bitch mother Chris later knew. Her psychic Trinity dictates the story while he listens and makes notes. Again, these are only the highlights of mother's story.

CHRIS'S MONOLOGUE FROM MOTHER

Superficially my childhood was rich, and I should have been thought to have everything—position, status, stable parents, intelligence, good looks. Actually, most of my life was hell. My dad was the son of poor parents and worked his way through medical school, working 20 hours a day much of the time. My mother was beautiful and married him for his position-to-be. They had me earlier than they were ready, while he was still struggling to start a practice. Mother was a social climber in a covert way, and Dad was aloof and demanding of himself. Mother was demanding of everyone. So I was born into their conflicts and frustrations.

Mother's family was more socially acceptable than Dad's, and when he hid out in his office and behind his medical journals, she turned her sharp tongue and ambitious eyes on me. I was her first born, looked like her and was expected to be like her.

People used to say how gracious Mother was, but I don't think so. She was as nasty as anybody, just slier about it. She worried about the impression I made, so I had to dress just so, even curtsy. I had to keep quiet and out of Dad's way when he had patients coming. Dad let Mom rule the house. I was often ashamed by his kowtowing to her. Men weren't supposed to be like that. But he was, and people outside the family never saw it. I don't know whether it was more Dad or Mom, but they used his profession to not relate to me. I might as well have been a robot myself or a puppet. Except I got to take it out on my sisters. Sister Lucy got her attention by being bad, cranky, loud, obnoxious. I had to try to get my love by conforming, being a goody-goody. I didn't have much chance with Mother's manipulating and rock-hard authoritarianism and Dad's moralistic withdrawal. They both spent lots of time invalidating me. Sometimes Mother pretended to listen, but she only used my feelings against me, demanding, shaming me, putting me down.

Things were especially tough when my next sister, Mary, was born. Mom said she was difficult, but she forced me to take responsibility for her. It wasn't till later that I wondered if she was by a different father, but of course that was *not* to be talked about. Dad was so shut off from talking with me, and maybe from his own feelings, I still don't know if he really wanted a boy. But I was always somehow aware that he was not with me. He let my mother raise me, and though he seemed to like the attention of us females, he never was close.

They couldn't even let me seek love elsewhere without constant warning about how others weren't as good as we were. God, I was lonely! When I wasn't lonely, I was angry and fearfully not showing it; angry at Dad for not taking time to listen to me, or for letting that controlling bitch mother shut me out. He had his work; I didn't have anything.

I wish Mother had had the humanity really to let go, hug me, touch me, be loving. But no, she was cold, aristocratic, aloof, and so smart that anything I tried to do to get attention either was doing her thing, not being myself, being a traitor to my own needs, or it backfired and brought angry criticism, with devastating looks or words. My parents gave credit for positive qualities only if they were the ones they decided on. I wanted credit for being me, their little girl.

Two of a kind they were: perfectionists, aloof, demanding, suppressed, unaffectionate, with duty before pleasure and adults before children. Yes, Chris, I guess you could call me the lonely, poor little rich girl.

After hearing what his mother, Eileen, has to tell him about her childhood, Chris is left with no doubt where, how, and why she became a Zombie who then programmed him to be a Zombie just like her. As he experiences emotionally how his mother adopted her negativities the way he adopted his, he begins to understand her without condemning her. He also learns there is no emotional need to cling to his false Zombie exterior and the other negative patterns that were not really hers any more than they are his.

After her own dialogue and monologue with mother, Nancy, too, is close to reaching the needed understanding with no condemnation and compassion for mother, as are Laura and Chris. It remains for Nancy to clean out the last remnants of anger and resentment by giving her negative emotional child permission for a final opportunity to speak out and have a second day in court. From time to time her spiritual self intervenes to help her accept the ultimate truth: Everyone is guilty, and no one is to blame.

NANCY'S TRIAL-LOG WITH MOTHER

> My child self, my spiritual self, and my mother's living spirit (newly aware) are in my sanctuary. The child is permitted and encouraged to vent any residual bitchiness, the spiritual self has awareness and authority to preside, and mother is imbued with understanding and the desire to explain.
>
> NANCY'S CHILD: I still hate you! I'm miserable, and it's all your fault.
>
> ADULT MOTHER: Yes, I can see that now. I was trying so hard to be a good mother, and actually I've been teaching you all the unhappiness and disappointment in life I learned from my own parents.
>
> NANCY'S CHILD: What good does it do me if you see it now? You should have seen what you were doing earlier. What right did you have to go around being so fucking sorry for yourself and teaching me self-pity?
>
> ADULT MOTHER: I felt sorry for myself, as my mother felt sorry for herself. I really believed that I was nothing if my man left me. That's how my mother felt, and I see now that I couldn't outdo her. I still wanted her love when I should have been mothering you.
>
> NANCY'S CHILD: Yah! You were nothing either way. I don't blame him for leaving you. You were self-righteous, critical, and a bad-tempered drag, anyway!
>
> SPIRITUAL SELF: Easy there, child. You know now how she got that way. In your talk with her 13-year-old you found out what her childhood was like.

NANCY'S CHILD: But all you ever did was *play* mother. Big dramatic scenes. Never there when I really needed you. Running me down while expecting *me* to build *you* up. Confused! Insecure! Afraid of other people! Damn you for all that, anyhow! You taught it to me.

ADULT MOTHER: Again, like my mother. She didn't believe she was as good as my father, or even as his sister. She felt put down by them both. But when he obviously preferred other women, the only hold she had on him, the only position she had in life, that of wife, came crashing down. I know now that through negative love I became just like her.

NANCY'S CHILD: And all that phony pretense you laid on me. The phony smiles, the lack of self-love. That's the worst! You had no real self, no self-respect, only that empty pride. You didn't love yourself!

ADULT MOTHER: I had no way of learning. My parents had no self-love, and my position as the third and unwanted girl, Henry coming along after me and being the son they wanted, left me with no right even to exist. I felt that I was somehow just tolerated because I was there, not because I had a right to be there.

NANCY'S CHILD: I won't feel sorry for you! You were a rotten, uncaring mother!

SPIRITUAL SELF: No one is asking you to feel sorry for her, child. Only to listen and to understand.

ADULT MOTHER: What my mother gave me was pseudo-love. I always felt that she was playing at being grown-up. She had no confidence in herself. The only way she got what she wanted was by getting my father or my aunt, and later her children, to give it to her.

NANCY'S CHILD: But all that repressed anger of yours and the wild outbursts of temper— You laid those on me. I walked on eggshells around you, you Goddamned volcano. I never knew when you'd blow off!

ADULT MOTHER: My father was always very distant with us as children and maintained his position as head of the house by keeping us in fear of him. We were too much in awe of him to treat him with anything but utmost respect openly. But he was a liar and a phony, and he resented us. We all knew he had a terrible temper and we were all afraid of arousing him. He was terribly critical of us all, while he was self-righteous about his own behavior. He felt himself superior to other people, and especially to my mother, but inside he was weak and phony. Don't you see that I adopted all that through negative love?

NANCY'S CHILD: I guess I do see. But the suffering? How did you learn to let yourself suffer that way, to have no self-caring?

ADULT MOTHER: Starting when I was about nine, and for several years after that, my father had a mistress. We weren't supposed to know, but everybody did. My mother was by turns hysterical and grief stricken. I heard my older sisters talking about it and imagined that my mother would become like my aunt, unwanted and without a man to support her, and I worried terribly about what would become of us all. Actually, my father did not desert us totally and continued to support us, but my mother suffered terribly over his neglect during those years.

NANCY'S CHILD: You actually had the same kind of father I did!

ADULT MOTHER: Yes, I married a man who was just like my father. My father had wanted to be a poet but had to work in an office all his life to support his four children. He'd fallen in love with my mother and married her, but later he felt trapped by her and resented her.

NANCY'S CHILD: So you learned resentment that way, I see. But where did you get your authoritarianism and anger?

ADULT MOTHER: From my father. He ruled us by putting us all down and insisting on being the only important person there.

NANCY'S CHILD: So you had no way to learn to be a woman and to enjoy sex?

ADULT MOTHER: No one told me about sex, or that it was all right to have a body, when I was a child. I just learned there was something frightening and bad about relations between men and women.

(My child self puts her hand quietly on mother's shoulder and shakes her head sadly.)

NANCY'S CHILD: I really do see, Mother. (She has tears in her eyes.) Poor Mother. You were just as caught in this negative love trap as I was.

As the Trial-log closes, Nancy understands that mother could not help herself any more than Nancy could. Nancy has again accused mother of teaching her the traits that devastated her life, as she did in the bitch session, but this time is ready to hear her mother's defense. Mother's answers to her questions, fully understood and heard by Nancy's Trinity, enable her to relinquish her anger toward mother and leave a space to replace it with positive emotions. This removal of the residual anger, putting compassion in its place, differs completely from simply Baygull forgiveness or Zombie denial of the anger. Now that she knows where the negativity came from, Nancy is free to let go of it all without blaming anyone, which is what she, Laura, and Chris did.

All three have been touched to the point of tears by their dialogue, Mother's Negative Emotional Autobiography, and their Trial-log. But this level of compassion, although genuine, is not enough to wash away completely the agony of the years of repressed hostility. The full flow of emotions, gut-level sobbing, must be evoked. Each of them must then live through a dramatic compassion scene for their mother, seeing her going to her grave with her negative emotional child still within, never having a chance to grow up and become a whole, truly loving human being.

CHRIS'S COMPASSION SCENE FOR MOTHER

I get home and my daughter tells me my mother has been killed in a traffic accident. I feel a sudden wrenching shock. I call my wife to come home and stay with the kids while I drive to the hospital. At the hospital I'm shown a gurney with a body covered by a sheet. Lifting the sheet, I see it's my mother—dead! I am stunned and feel sick. I ask to be alone with her for a few minutes. Sitting next to her body, I take her cold hand in mine and think of the promises I've made to spend more time to get to know her. I think especially of this process, which is giving me the chance to change so I can actually express love for her. At the funeral home the next day I look inside her with psychic x-ray vision and see her child, scared, hurt, never developed. I gently place a single red rose on her breast and see the little hands of her pathetic negative child reaching to clutch it. (Tears.) She never became a woman, never had a chance really to be a mother to me or anyone else. Now I'll never get to know her. She'll never really know me, her only son. (More tears.)

Later, at the graveside, I look at her coffin and feel the heavy weight of sadness for that unloved, unloving, never-grown child in her. She had such an empty 74 years. I was such a stingy, insensitive, scared son. (Cried some more, on and off, through much of this typing.) Oh, Mother, you had 74 (it probably seemed like 174) years! I've had 46 with you, and we've never really been able to love each other. (Sobbing.) Why did you have to die just when that damn negative love chain was being broken, when I might have learned to love you? We never even knew each other. We had so much in common and so little love.

Don't die yet. I *will* be free! I *will* learn to love! I'll become a loving son and fulfill you even though you couldn't fulfill me. Mother, don't be dead! (More sobbing.)

With these words of sadness and longing, Chris ended his work with mother for the moment. He had not yet learned to love her, but he had freed himself of his deeply repressed anger while achieving a genuinely compassionate understanding for her. She's no longer a bitch, and he's no longer a Zombie. Instead, he is more expressive and animated both in his writing and his facial expressions and body posture. In short, he is far more alive and alert than he was only a few short weeks before.

The changes in the others at this time were equally dramatic, although of a different nature. Nancy became softer and more approachable to other people. Laura lost some of her Baygull sweetness and replaced it with a more straightforward demeanor. She continued to smile, but less often and more convincingly. All of them were far more real than ever before in their adult lives. They were on their way.

The Defense of Mother proves that negative love is like a locked cage, and intellect is not the key. No amount of intellectual "knowing" about her childhood experiences can create compassion for her. To give up blaming her is not just an intellectual decision but a deeply felt emotional commitment. You must experience her life, or "walk a mile in her shoes," to paraphrase an American Indian saying, to find compassion for her.

Once you have experienced mother as an unloved little girl, you will never again see her in the same way. The Bitch is no more. In her place is a child of the Godhead, just like you and everyone else. She is guilty, but not to blame, for your childhood misery. When you can feel for mother as a real person victimized by negative love, you are closer to becoming an autonomous, loving human being, free at last of her puppet strings that have controlled your life.

8. "Go to Hell, Daddy!"

If your mother was a bitch, your father was a bastard. His failure to fulfill your mother in their marriage lies at the center of the entire constellation of family problems you knew as a child. The arguing, coldness, abandonment, withdrawal, the false smiles and dishonest communication—however unlovingness was expressed in your home, your father's failure as a husband and father was the source. If he was not the strong central figure in the family, exuding confidence, emotional stability, and warmth, everyone suffered, particularly your mother. If she was bitter and unloving, look to your father, who failed to create a loving atmosphere in the home. Having a husband she cannot love and respect is the ultimate heartbreak and frustration for a woman.

Most people have less difficulty seeing father as negative because overcoming the barriers against full awareness of mother during her Prosecution prepares the way to do the same during father's Prosecution. Also, father, more often than mother, is the villain in the childhood recollections. He was usually the more obviously powerful one in the home, and also the more distant. Men in Western culture have traditionally been expected to provide for their families and be the rock on which the family can depend. Women have been expected to be warm but not as strong as men. Children in our society become aware quite early of these differences in the responsibilities of men and women and usually expect more of their fathers than of their mothers. Children also feel more bitterness and resentment toward father when he fails them.

The Prosecution and Defense of Father is like that of mother in almost all respects. To be free of father's negative influence, you must first recognize his negative traits by seeing the childhood scenes in which he expressed them with you. Putting these scenes in chronological order serves to concentrate and focus the full awareness on father's negativity and how it has contributed to your adult problems. Writing the Negative Emotional Autobiography with Father returns you to the negative space needed to prepare for the bitch session with father. As with mother, the full fury of the anger and resentment from childhood must be experienced and released in order to be free of its negative influence.

The vividness and detail of the childhood recall of these clients is not at all unusual. Mind revelations and other psychic techniques make it possible for everyone to break through the blocks that have cut them off from crucial early events.

While directing attention to father's negative traits helps to incite the anger that is always present beneath the surface, his positive traits, like those of mother, are also a source of emotional difficulty. The positive traits are an example against which an angry child may rebel to gain revenge or negative attention. If father is punctual, for example, the negative emotional child may show his angry face to father through procrastination. The real-life consequences of procrastination (lost friends, lost time, lost income) will be heaped atop the conflict he already feels over deviating from father's example. The conflict itself stems from feeling two powerful, contradictory emotions at the same time: anger and guilt. He feels furiously angry with father for not loving him as he knows love was meant to be expressed. And he feels desperately guilty and ashamed for deliberately not becoming like father. "You don't love me, so I won't love you," says the negative emotional child within the rebel. In so doing, he defies his two strongest emotional urges: to love and be loved.

How much more painful is the conflict when father's positive traits are opposite to mother's negative traits. Now the child has severe conflict problems, for obeying mother means disobeying father, and vice versa. If mother rarely did things on schedule, for example, and father always did, their child will act confused and indecisive. He also may struggle in vain against his time management problems without ever understanding their real cause.

As they did with mother, clients prepare to bitch at father by reviewing their list of his negative traits, moods, and admonitions, both silent and overt. They are shocked to discover that they are the bastard father all over again by adopting his negative traits as their own. Even though they have already seen it with mother, people are always amazed and surprised to see how like their (negative) fathers they really are. Their anguish is further complicated because the few positive traits of father's are often directly opposite to mother's negative traits, while the few positive traits of mother's are offset by the opposite negative traits in father. "Damned if you do, and damned if you don't" describes the double conflict exactly.

Tallying father's negative traits and honestly deciding how you responded to them (adoption or rebellion) has the same enraging effect as doing it with mother. And as before a mere intellectual understanding will not do. The anger has to be from the gut.

What kind of father did you have? How was his relationship with mother during your embryo period? How did father feel about mother being pregnant with you? Did he look forward to your addition to the family? Or were you a surprise and a burden, unwanted even before you were born?

Are you the sex your father wanted you to be? Or did you disappoint him? If you were the son he wanted, did he treat you as his heir apparent, expecting you to make your life the fulfillment of all the ambitions he never achieved? Or was he jealous of you, teaching you never to be better at anything than he was? Did he give you the admonition, "Don't outdo me"? Even now, do you see your strengths and weaknesses only by comparing yourself with him? Or do you see yourself as separate from him?

Perhaps you were a daughter instead of the son he wanted. How did he deal with your femaleness? Did he ignore you, teaching you that only men counted? Or did he cover his negative feelings toward you, his daughter, by offering you pseudo-love? What did Daddy's example of manhood teach you about men? That they are cold and distant? Or perhaps Daddy's weakness and immaturity taught you that men are overgrown babies needing constant attention? Either way, he cheated you of your right to see and experience an example of properly developed manhood to prepare you to be an adult woman.

When you were an infant, did father only play with you when he felt like it? Or was he aware of your need for his loving attention at all times? Did he arrange his life to be able to meet your need? Or did he put his own needs ahead of yours? If he played with you when you were happy, did he also attend to you when you were wet, or sick, or otherwise less than beautiful? Or was he a fair-weather father, only interested in you when you didn't ask anything in return?

Later, when you were old enough to run after him, did he give you his time and attention when you needed it? Or did he brush you off with a pat on the head or perhaps an angry rebuke for intruding on him? If he had loved to love he would have spent a great deal of time with you in your childhood. Had he wanted, he could have gotten more fulfillment and positive energy by giving his love to you and receiving it from you than by retreating into a nap or taking a drink. Instead of giving a loving, consistent flow of communication, did he cop out on you? When did Daddy hold you in his arms and give you his love?

Did father share with mother in your upbringing? Or did he let her decide how you were to be cared for? Was he just a meal ticket and policeman, while giving no warmth and direction to your childhood? If so, he cheated you of the loving masculine contribution necessary to your development.

Your attitudes toward women come directly from the way your father felt about your mother. What was your father's attitude toward your mother? Did he respect and admire her as an example of womanhood? Or did he run her down to build himself up, thus teaching you not to respect women? Or did he put your mother on a pedestal, teaching you that women are everything and men are nothing?

What kind of greeting did your father give your mother? When he came home in the evening (assuming that he *did* come home) did he take her in his arms and caress her tenderly so that she knew she was cared for, wanted, and loved? Or did he drag himself in the door, give her a perfunctory nod or a dutiful peck on the cheek, and retreat to the television or behind a newspaper? If so, he is the one responsible for your mother becoming the disappointed, angry, castrating woman you knew. His distance, coldness, and indifference drained her of her emotional goodness and aggravated her negativity. It was father's responsibility to melt the iceberg.

Father's warmth needs to extend beyond mother to include the children. When father came home, did he kiss mother but ignore you? Did you feel rejected and left out? Did you say to yourself something like, "OK for you, Daddy. If you won't love me, I won't love you."? If so, he's the one who is responsible for your continuing to feel left out and rejected by others or to reject others before they reject you. Both patterns of unfulfillment come from father's stupidity in not including you in the love circle.

How did father wield his power as head of the house? Was he a tyrant, angrily insisting that things be his way or else? Did everyone have to arrange their lives to suit his taste? Did he insist on silence at the dinner table, thus stifling any loving communication during these moments the family was together? Did he hold sway over your mother so that she was little more than his servant? Did he teach you to be sullenly compliant while secretly resentful? Your attitude toward men in power derives from the way you saw father exercise his power over you and your mother.

Or was father a weakling who gave in to everyone? When mother disagreed with him, did he just nod and say, "Yes, dear. Whatever you say, dear."? Did father teach you to avoid "making waves" so that even today you dare not disagree openly with anyone?

Did your father allow your mother to emasculate him? If so, he taught you to see men as weaklings dominated by women. If she ran the house and everyone in it, it's his fault for not being the loving adult male every household needs to be complete. If he cannot stand up to her, how will she respect his manhood and feel love toward him? Every married woman, whether she helps support the family financially or not, wants to know that the man she has thrown in her lot with can be counted on to "be there" emotionally for her. She needs to know his strength, and that she can trust his loving manhood, that she can depend upon him to complement her own essence. She also needs to feel accepted by him as an equal, rather than dismissed as an inferior to be exploited. For warmth and emotional goodness to exist and prosper between them, husband and wife must be mates on an equal basis.

Was he also inconsistent in his love and warmth for you and your brothers and sisters? Did you feel tolerated by him, sensing that he often wished you weren't around? Were you just a mouth to feed? Did he praise your achievements as well as correct your errors? Or did you get mostly negative attention from him, thus learning that the way to get him to notice you was to break something or make a mistake? Are you still goofing off today, at home and at work, to continue to get father's negative attention? If so, all that negativity is a horrible pattern your bastard father taught you.

Did your father teach you to get along well with your brothers and sisters? Or did he make you compete for his love, thus teaching you resentment and jealousy for one another? Father should have played an important part in presenting you to the other children in the family so that no sibling rivalry developed, as described in Chapter 5.

Which kind of discipline did father use on you? The cast-iron fist, the limp wrist, or the firm, loving hand? Did he use punishment fairly as a means to help you learn? Or did he use it cruelly? Was he so wrapped up in his own concerns that he didn't bother to teach you right from wrong? If your father had been a loving man, he would have disciplined you lovingly.

When your father did spend time with you, what did you do together? Who decided how you would spend the time? Did you do only the things he wanted to do? Or did you do things he thought were "good for you"? Or was he so guilty over his failure to really love you that he always let you do whatever you wanted? A loving father is flexible, neither controlling his children totally nor leaving them without guidance.

If your father had money, was he generous with it? Did he teach you to see money as a means to gain necessities and a few luxuries? Or did he use money to buy you off with presents that were really bribes and guilt offerings? Did he give you a regular allowance and teach you to manage money? Or did he make you go begging to him every time you wanted to buy something for yourself? As you grew old enough to understand, did he inform you of the family's financial affairs? Or did he keep you in the dark so that you would never be able to question his decisions or learn to make your own?

If the family was well-off, did he buy household help who saw to your daily upbringing, thus relieving him of any responsibility to you? If so, he was your father in a biological sense only, a man who was there but not there, like a phantom father.

What about giving him gifts on special days? Did he appreciate your thoughtfulness in choosing something to please him? Or was he unresponsive to your gifts, leaving you with the feeling that nothing you could give him would please him? Did your father teach you not to show him any love by refusing your gifts as tokens of that love?

What did your father do when you brought home your report card from school? Was he indifferent to your grades? Or did he have expectations that were impossible for you to meet? Did he insist that only straight A's were good enough for *his* child? Or did he send you the message that you were stupid, thus ensuring that you would never develop your full ability? Did he punish you for low marks while ignoring you when you did well? If you are still getting more negative than positive attention, you can look to your bastard father as the cause.

Was father a Don Juan who had to make it with all the women in sight in order to prove his masculinity? If so, he neglected your need for real love while pursuing his neurotic urge to quell his doubts about his manhood.

What kind of worker was father? Did he work compulsively from early morning until late at night, so that you hardly ever saw him except when he was too tired to give you any loving attention? Or was he shiftless and unreliable, so that you were in constant fear of financial insecurity? Was his life a healthy mixture of work and leisure? If not, he failed you in several ways. A child needs to see an example of a balanced life in order to know how to create one for himself.

Did your father know the difference between being a father and being a friend? Did he try to buddy up to you and be your pal to impress you with what a "great guy" he was? Companionship is great, but children need a loving adult father, not an aging playmate.

Did your father demand, however subtly, that you live up to his expectations of you? Did he insist that you go to college or graduate school, or perhaps enter a particular profession, in order to fulfill his frustrated ambitions from 30 years ago? Did he want you to be what he never had the time, money, or opportunity to become? Many children have been ruined in their adult vocations because they were forced into a career they didn't want. Others have spent their working lives far below their potential because they rebelled against their parents' oppressive manipulations and demands for achievement.

Did your father have a sense of humor? How much did he laugh, and what kind of laugh was it? Jolly? Sarcastic? Mocking? Phony? Was he able to laugh at himself as well as at others? Were there any subjects he took too seriously ever to laugh at? Or was he a sourpuss who thought humor was silly and childish? A humorless father is a terrible curse. If your father never laughed with you, he destroyed much of your natural capacity for fun and pleasure.

How did father fulfill his responsibility for your sexual education? Did father take the time to prepare you for your sexual adulthood? Did he help you understand the meaning of your first menstrual period or your first ejaculation? How did he make you aware you were about to become a biological and physiological adult? What did he do to help you *feel* like a man or a woman?

What did he tell you about adult sexuality? Have you found what he told you to be true and helpful, or was he passing along misinformation and prejudices from his childhood? What would it be like to live in a world filled with men who are sexually like your father?

Did father die in your early childhood? If so, he deserted you, for death is desertion. It is necessary to prosecute such a father because there are still negative traits one adopts through hearsay or having actually experienced them in early childhood. If mother never remarried, then father's desertion in death left you without a father or a father image. If father actually deserted you and abandoned you, then he is definitely guilty of creating the rejection pattern in you that says, "I'm not good enough to be loved by father or by men."

If mother did remarry, what kind of stepfather did you have? The stepfather is then the father surrogate, and all the rude questions about father apply to your stepfather as well.

As with mother, father's acts of omission are as important as his acts of commission. Were there areas of father-child life about which he said or did nothing? Whatever he ignored or overlooked has left a gaping hole in your development as a complete adult, either male or female.

If you have not already done it, now is the time to take father off that pedestal you may have put him on. Whether you have been aware of it or not, he is responsible for most of your life problems. Your father's many failings as a man, husband, and father are a major source of your deepest anxieties, conflicts, and frustrations. Until you purge yourself of him, you will remain a prisoner of your negative love for him.

What kind of father did you have?

After a lecture based on these questions and a mind revelation to aid in their recall, Chris, Nancy, and Laura were ready to write the Negative Emotional Autobiography with Father and to experience father's bitch sessions. As with mother, only excerpts from their notes are given here.

By the time he finished his mother work, Chris had evolved sufficiently to enable him to express his feelings more openly. He was still blocked in many areas, though, because he had received an even larger dose of Zombie programming from his father than from his mother. After recalling 135 negative traits for his father, (a well-known Protestant minister), he went back into his childhood and found the scenes in which his father displayed them. Not surprisingly, Chris found that his father's negative traits, (such as authoritarian, manipulative, uncaring, nonsupportive, critical, judgmental, invalidator, and many others), were a crucial influence in his emotional development during childhood. The few instances in which Chris rebelled against his father were either insignificant or unsuccessful, leading only to painful conflict.

Chris had become a Zombie adult as the result of what we call a double compound fracture, when one adopts the same negative trait or admonition from both parents.

CHRIS, THE ZOMBIE

When I was born, my father was in the process of fulfilling his idea of the way his life should be, which set the stage for the rest of my life with him. He hoped to manipulate, mold, and shape me to what he wanted and expected of me. When he couldn't, he showed disappointment and withdrew from me. He knew duty but love was only on "giving-to-get" terms. When he didn't get, he went off to his world audience and to his "good works."

Father was a large man, active and full of self-importance. He used to encourage me to play, but on his terms. I remember at age 3 at the beach I was to run to the water with him. I was afraid, so he made fun of me. My feelings weren't real; his were. His message was "Keep quiet and conform" by denying and invalidating myself.

The major theme running all through my life with my father was his nonsupport of me, my feelings, my needs. By direct or subtle means, his manipulation and authoritarianism structured my life. His indifference and neglect left me lonely and longing.

Dad was often the center of attention at gatherings, a fine singer, a good storyteller, and knowledgeable in discussions of world and religious affairs. Somehow I was always excluded. The son of a bitch gave lots of attention to everybody in his congregation but me.

He always seemed busy. After work he'd say hello, give a dutiful hug and kiss to my mother but usually not to me. I felt left out. I wanted a hug and kiss, too. I wanted to talk to him. He'd sit and read his newspaper until dinner, where conversation was limited to his ministry or the family, about teaching me geography or vocabulary, or there were arguments over trivia. After dinner, either he went upstairs, closed his door, and worked on sermons (to instruct the world on how to love and have better marriages and raise children), or I was shuffled upstairs so he could give attention to a parishioner while I wasn't even permitted to come down to the kitchen for milk.

I learned how to hide my feelings early, certainly before age 5. I decided: Don't trust him with my real perceptions or feelings, or he will invalidate them. He might rob me of those most precious experiences. He claimed to know better than I did what I felt, thought, and needed.

Dad was especially good working with people, for which he got lots of acclaim. I rebelled at his hypocrisy and began to dislike people. I withdrew into myself and became interested in mechanical things and science, where I could work alone. Dad had no interest in these pursuits. He was disappointed because I wasn't a leader in the neighborhood. I didn't play football or baseball well enough to lead the older and bigger boys, and father never took the time to teach me how to play better.

I often got his message: Be manly. Don't show hurt, fear, or be overemotional. When I was 8, I fell off the garage roof while showing off to get his attention. He carried me back to the house to help me get my wind back but showed no sympathy or warmth. Or when I cut my knee four inches to the bone, he carried me to the car and kept saying, "Be a big boy. Don't cry." I was glad he came to get me, but he blamed me for hurting myself and made me swallow my tears. He always inhibited my honest emotions, and I have had trouble in this area ever since.

My memory of one of my strongest, deepest moments of desperation and sorrow was probably duplicated many times. I am standing outside the door of Dad's bedroom where he is preparing a speech. I very much want and need his attention and love and have asked him something. I want him to share my excitement about a school accomplishment. Impatiently he says, "Stop, you're disturbing me. I have a lecture to work on. Now don't bother me again." I feel crushed. My head says, "He has work to do." My guts shout, "I'm worthless, he doesn't love me, never takes time. I only wanted a little bit of his time." But he wouldn't take two minutes for his only son.

He was manipulative and dishonest in his approach to me. He didn't respect me enough to be straight, though often I saw through it and was hurt and felt contempt for him. He gave me a sex book but did not share feelings about sex, manhood, warmth, or father-son contact.

My parents never openly disagreed or argued. She gave in on almost everything. He "knew" it wasn't good for a child to hear his parents arguing. Just as I was excluded from his warmth and love, so I was excluded from seeing people honestly disagree and still get along. I still experience disagreement as dangerous and threatening, thanks to my unfatherly father.

My strongest experience with my father was when I was about 11. He had been trying to get me to gain weight. (I wasn't OK as I was.) He decided I wasn't gaining because I was bad, deficient, lazy, unmotivated. I must gain one-half pound a day. Every morning for what seemed like months I was weighed and given a bare-assed swat for each one-half pound below his chart. I tried to gain, but I got sick. I would get up at five in the morning and drink quantities of water, fight not to vomit it all up, and go back to bed to appear asleep when he woke up. He felt guilty, so he told me he wanted to lose weight (true) and set a goal of losing one pound a day. For each pound he was over, I was to swat him bare-assed with a bed slat. I knew he was doing that to ease his own guilt. I didn't want to hit my father—I still wanted to respect him—but when he insisted I hit him, I wanted to bash his Goddamned head to a bloody pulp. When he wouldn't let me out of the room until I did spank him, I finally would bash his ass as hard as I could, but it really didn't feel good. I wanted to shout how I hated his fucking guts right then, but I knew I was too scared.

The crowning blow, his abandonment of me and ultimate cop-out, was that he killed himself before my puberty by continuing to be overweight, ignoring his physician's statement that his heart was in critical condition. He worked long hours every day and had a heart attack in his pulpit, ironically telling people how to live happy lives, conduct happy marriages, and love one another. He didn't even have the decency to die at home.

To be able to cut the strings to your parents and find autonomy, you must first re-experience the stage at which you yearned for and needed their total love and support, along with the deep sense of loneliness and loss that comes from not getting it. Chris's father had manipulated him into denying his view of the world and what he felt about what he saw.

His father taught Chris he must never cry or show honest emotions, as in the incident when Chris fell off the garage and injured himself. When it came time for Chris to throw off his father's programming, I made a point of encouraging him to cry the tears his father had made him hold back. By letting the tears flow, Chris was already beginning to rid himself of his father's negative programming.

The feedback to Chris's father's work is similar in design and intent to the feedback on mother. Paragraph by paragraph Chris is made to see the overwhelming injustice and unlovingness in his father's treatment of him as a child. As a Zombie, Chris was trained to be dead to the emotional unreality of his life. The feedback serves to help jolt him out of his lassitude and unresponsiveness into anger at his bastard father.

"You want to be loved," I said, "and your bastard father denied you your inalienable right to be loved by your parents. He really was a bastard father because it is already obvious that you were not important to him."

"He ignored your existence," I told him angrily on the tape. "You were only his puppet. Hell, Chris, you needed a loving father to depend on and look up to, not the puppeteer you had."

"The spanking episode showed he was a sado-masochist. Are you one now? That bastard's treatment of you at home was selfish and cruel. While presenting himself to the world as the benevolent, magnanimous church man, he ran his home like an intellectual tyrant. Did he 'rule' with the firm hand of loving discipline? Certainly not. There was no loving manliness in his domination of the household. In truth he was a terribly unloving man who didn't trust others unless he was sure he could control their every move. Though he was supposed to be an authority on the heart of man and lectured to parents on how to love their children, he was himself no better than those he professed to lead. It was really a case of the blind leading the blind, since he was a nothing father."

If some of these words sound harsh and hurtful, they were intended to be. There had to be no doubt in Chris's mind that his father was a bastard who did a pathetic job of raising him. Like the cobbler's son who goes barefoot, Chris was the minister's son starved for love. His father was so busy buying the world's approval for his words of loving wisdom that he made no time to practice what he preached. Again and again I reminded Chris that in the name of God's love his father had denied him a father's love. He never gathered the boy in his arms, kissed him and told him everything was all right, that Dad was there to love him and take care of him. Instead, Chris was brought up by a cold, unemotional, admonishing bastard.

Feedback like this evokes the anger a Zombie like Chris needed to get so flaming angry that he would spit out all that he had been holding down against father for more than 30 years. Primed as he was by the painful memories in the Negative Emotional Autobiography, Chris had little trouble moving immediately to the bitch session. Afterward, he wrote his reaction to the first bitch session and transcribed the tape of a second bitch session on his own.

"Monday night, after throwing up in the actual bitch session, I felt some releaf, I mean relief (good slip, 'leaf' as in healthy tree growth), also relieved at having expressed the inexpressible, vomited the unvomitable, and having generally recovered from the intensified sickness of the bitch session plus some riddance of the daddy-tied feeling. Today, Wheeeee!"

Here is a portion of his transcribed bitch session done the next day on his own:

> You bastard! I've been scared of you. I've been scared of people, scared of you—but no more! I'm not scared of you now. What do you think of that, you bastard?
>
> You *made me scared,* you authoritarian fucker. Telling me, "Leave me alone" or "Go see Mother." My mother could have been a woman. She could have loved me . . . if you had cared . . . and had any balls . . . all you needed to do was love her and love me, listen to us, show us you cared. You'd come home . . . home! . . . That's supposed to be where there's *caring.* You'd come home, pick up your Goddamn paper, talk to mother, say to me, "Hello, how was your day?" and you'd walk out while I was telling you. You were supposed to listen, weren't you?
>
> You went out to get loved by the world because you couldn't take it from me. The only way I could get your attention was to screw up. You went off and you'd leave me. I hate your Goddamn guts. I'd like to kill you!
>
> All I wanted from you was warmth. I wanted you to see me. (Crying) I wanted you just to sit down and see what it was I was doing; give me credit. But no, you shit! You didn't have the time. You and your crusade to save the world for love, you phony fucker! (Crying)
>
> Afraid of how other people would judge you, eh? You didn't care how I judged you. Well I judge you now: a nothing No Thing . . . No Person. *No father. Nothing.* Self-centered, exhibitionistic zero! Big man! I was 10 years old, and you put me down for not beating you up. Maybe that's what you wanted? That *is* what you wanted, Goddamn it! Well, it's what I want to do now. Then I didn't want to beat you. You intimidated me, and you shamed me,

and you scared me, and you made me beat you on the butt with that Goddamned board, and the only thing I wanted was love. I didn't want to hit you . . . (Crying) . . . I wanted you to care.

I hate you so fucking much! Well now I've got me a way to get it out. I'm going to throw up. I'm going to throw you up, as I couldn't do all those years. "Don't cry, be a man." Do you remember that? You didn't tell me not to throw up. No, you'd just spank me if I lost weight. And if I threw up all that water I was drinking, I'd lose weight. You taught me . . . you taught me to keeeeeeep down all that shit. *No more.* You can be what you are for the next hundred years . . . stink in it . . . no more for me . . . no more . . . I've had enough.

Intellectualizing son of a bitch! I'm going to get you out of me for good . . . and I will not let you back in. No, no, not ever again . . . no more. I won't let you in again, you shit!

After I finished, I went to my sanctuary and my child looked down at my "father" who is still tied, curled up and protecting his head, bruised, quiet. On my instruction, my guide drags him/it bodily out. I thought about helping drag it, but realized I really didn't want to get that close to the S.O.B. now. He's left still tied on the ground outside as my guide and I shut the door together. I find I am breathing deeply of the air in my sanctuary and this time feeling really relieved. My legs are still shaking, and I feel weak, but God do I feel more solid, more my own man, stiff and sore muscles, but lighter and freer somehow.

When you get the hate out in the open like this and clear it, you can do far more than dutifully follow the Biblical admonition to honor your father. You can indeed learn to love him honestly.

NANCY, THE HOSTILE

Nancy saw less of her father during her childhood than Chris saw of his, but she was nonetheless emotionally devastated by the negative impact he had on her. For her father, who deserted the family when she was 3, she found 71 negative traits, moods, and admonitions. She adopted 46 of father's negative traits and rebelled against the other 25. Until she wrote her Negative Emotional Autobiography with Father and heard my feedback, she believed her father had been only a minor influence in her life, since she had only vague memories of him. In fact, her father played an important role in her negative development, particularly in the development of her anger and hostility. Her father's angry moods were more overt than those of her mother and dominated the household atmosphere. Her father was also the source of the message that her mother and all women (including Nancy herself), were worthless and that it was a woman's lot in life to be abandoned by men. She rejected herself because of her father's rejection of her and married two men who shared her father's negative attitude toward women. In these excerpts from her Negative Emotional Autobiography with Father, Nancy realizes how traumatic had been their brief time together and how, through the negative love pattern, her father continued to be the dominant force in her adult life. After returning psychically to the time before her birth, she wrote:

> My father was surprised when my mother told him she was pregnant. He had been ignoring her, involved in his business, going to whorehouses because he'd lost interest in her. So he was dismayed and worried about the likely expenses. She'd had a terrible time giving birth to my brothers, and he considered my existence an inescapable evil in a life full of irritations.
>
> When I was first born, he paid no attention to me at all except for a feeling of relief that it had been an easy birth after all, and my mother could now get back to her duties without too much difficulty, and his life wouldn't be disrupted too much. I yearned for my daddy, but he quite literally never touched me or spoke to me until I was past a year old. I would feel his presence sometimes, nodding approvingly, making phony affectionate sounds since I was never presented to him unless I was dressed up. He talked about me, though, and admired me as the "baby," and immediately insisted that my 3-year-old brother have his hair cut short and start acting and be disciplined like a boy

since he was no longer the baby in the family. That resulted in my brother Walter's resenting me violently all his life.

When I started to be responsive and walk around, he began occasionally to pet me and play with me as one would with a puppy or kitten. When he was in the mood, I would be swung up on his broad shoulders and feel his warmth. I would be his darling and his baby, and he became so terribly important to me! He was full of strength and vitality. But it was a seesaw love. Available sometimes, for reasons I didn't understand, then not there. I'd imagine that I had done something wrong to lose him, that there was something wrong with me.

There were few open quarrels between him and my mother in those days. Mostly I remember his bad temper, his demandingness, his disinterest in her as a person, and her hurt silences and tears in the night. I knew Daddy didn't love either of us.

As a businessman he was downright stupid, mostly brought on by his bullheaded conviction that he was always right and his decisions had to be correct. He had difficulty supporting us, changing jobs often. He had so much anger in him that he was often into battles with those he worked with. We had to move three times before I was 3—always to worse places—following his different jobs. There was never a feeling of security in the home. He was moody, irritable, subject to unexplained changes that would throw the whole family into a new environment. I was scared of him so often.

But he was sometimes loving to me, and as I grew a little older, I was delightedly conscious of my special place as his pet, and I adored and feared him at the same time. On the Christmas just before I was 3 he made a wooden slide in the basement for my brother and me. I was proudly given the first ride, lifted to the top by him. I ran a large splinter into my behind. He had wanted to give us something impressive, but he hadn't even been careful enough to see that we wouldn't be hurt on it. He laid me over his knee and took it out, and I was aware of my mother's anger at him and my own pain and his being the source of it, and feeling confused and torn up inside not wanting to be away from him, anyway.

Then we packed up for a long trip to Wisconsin. Just the three kids and my mother went. We were to enter my brothers in school, and he was going to join us as soon as his present business venture permitted because he was going to work in Wisconsin. He kissed me and hugged me and said he'd be coming real soon, and I believed him.

He never came. One thing after another held him up, and the years went by. He never even came to visit. He didn't send enough money to support us, and my mother had to go to work. He abandoned us. He didn't want us. The stupid, insensitive, uncaring bastard!! He was so involved in himself, so convinced of his own importance that he could rationalize his treatment of us. And he knew that my mother was a child emotionally and couldn't take care of us. He just didn't care. He knew she couldn't earn more than starvation wages. He knew how unhappy she was and that we had to live with that. All his warmth and lovingness toward me had been a lie. He didn't really care at all.

When I was 5½, my mother determined to go back and force him to take on his family again. When we got to the house where he was living, my mother sent me ahead to announce our arrival. After recovering from the shock, he did pick me up to hug me. I felt a clutching in my throat, so I turned my head away as I'd been taught, not to cough in his face. He didn't understand, and we had a brief tussle, him pulling me toward him, my pulling away. Then he set me down in dismissal, and I never got to be hugged or kissed. I know now I couldn't handle my yearning for him and rage at his having left us.

So we all moved in together, and unpleasant scenes between him and my mother punctuated our days. We all knew that he liked some other woman better than my mother. I could hear it in his voice, and sense it in his actions. And I was no longer his pet; his response to me was merely perfunctory. At first I yearned so for him to pay attention to me, but he simply acted as if I were one more female too many. He gave my brothers each a puppy, and I was supposed to be content with the kitten my aunt brought me six weeks later. He took my brothers on an outing to the Statue of Liberty, and I had to spend the day in my aunt's lamp shop. I learned from him then what a disaster it is to be female, how much I missed out on because I wasn't one of his sons.

Once my mother told my brothers to do the dishes, and my father announced grandly that he was going to be a millionaire—and the sons of a millionaire did not have to do dishes. What about the wife of a millionaire? What about the daughter of a millionaire?

Once I was under the kitchen table when my father came into the room. I stayed there, hidden, shaking with fear and hating him as he yelled at my mother, pounding on the table with his fist.

A little while after that my mother and brothers and I moved again. I don't even remember saying good-bye to him. I was scared of the unknown we were going into but glad to be leaving him. I hated him. I didn't want to be around him anymore.

From that time on we were alone. The communication, if any, between him and my mother was a mystery to me. I received no word from him, not so much as a card on my birthday or on Christmas.

Five years later, back in New York, my mother tried to force him to help support us. There was some kind of court scene. I remember sitting outside with my brother, and I saw him go in. I made no effort to speak to him and turned my head away. I never saw him again after that. He died when I was 17, and I didn't attend his funeral because we were in California by then. I didn't want to, anyhow.

In response to Nancy's father work I validated her perception and supported her new understanding that her father's uncaring behavior had devastating results for everyone in the family. (In this regard, the feedback serves not only to heighten awareness but also to confirm the reality of what the client thinks she sees.) She had been a pretty little girl, I told her, and would one day be a beautiful woman when she rid herself of the morose, neglected look her father had left her with.

Although she hardly needed much reminding, I stressed again and again what a rotten, no-good bastard her father had been to her and the rest of the family; how his angry behavior planted the seeds of her insecurity and lack of self-assurance, particularly around men. At my urging she went more deeply into the scenes of her father angrily pounding the table and yelling, which served to focus her anger on his loud, violent assaults on the family's serenity. I used the incident with the splinter in her buttocks to demonstrate her evident masochism in relating to men. With a little help and some honest introspection she saw that she liked to be hurt by men in order to continue to relate negatively to her father.

"He was a penny-ante Hitler," I said to her on tape. "A big Daddy-O, a real zero who insisted his wife and children walk on eggshells. He put you on a seesaw of love, giving you an occasional thrill and then dropping you on your emotional ass. Because of that bastard you never knew which end was up, and you still don't!"

Beyond these feelings of his treatment toward her, I called her on her mistaken belief that it would have been better to have been a son to this bastard father of hers. I reminded her that her brothers had been in terrible emotional shape all their lives because of his treatment of them, that her misfortune was not that she was born a female but that she was fathered by a scoundrel and a bully. In every possible way I encouraged her to see her father as he really was in all his negativity. Her anger and resentment steadily rose to fever pitch and burst forth on the bitch night and for the week thereafter.

At the end of her bitch session with father, Nancy wrote, "I'm going down in the basement now and get a brick, and mark your face in the dirt, and pound on it until I feel through. I went down and made a face in the dirt—your face, with eyes and mouth, and pounded on it with a brick until it was just a bloody pulp, and then I made it your balls and smashed them, and then I set up your face again and smashed it once for my mother who mourned you all of her life. And then I was finished. I came upstairs and vomited and felt that I was vomiting you from out of every cell of my body."

At my suggestion Nancy also did a brief scene in which her guide brought her father into her sanctuary for a final moment before she rid herself of him. Then her guide helped her begin to recover from the exertions of the bitching:

> "I am in my sanctuary. My guide sends out my adult intellectual self, leaving the negative child at age 13. He pro-

duces father, immobilized. My first reaction is to spit in his face. Then I think of Bob's suggestion to vomit on him, and I do. It comes from my toes, streams and streams of vile-looking yellowish and greenish gunk. It goes on and on, finally leaving me empty and white and shaken. My guide removes my father and helps me out of my soiled clothes. First I wash off in the nearby ocean, and then we go to my healing pool. I feel tears in my eyes as my guide walks with his arm supportively around my shoulders. He bathes me in the healing pool, washing my hair and letting water run from his cupped palm over my face in a half-playful fashion. Afterward he gives me a costume of soft, clean blue, like the one he gave me at our first meeting. I rest in the sun. My adult self quietly joins me.

LAURA, THE BAYGULL

Like Nancy and all other little girls, Laura's first male love in life had been her father. Her emotional life as a woman was blighted, though, because her father never returned the love she instinctively felt for him. While she had been painfully aware of his rejection of her, which is evident in her recollections of their life together, she believed she had rejected him in return. The truth of her negative love for him appeared to her only after she compiled his list of more than 400 negative traits and realized she had adopted 325 of them into her personality. She was her father all over again! These excerpts from her story of their relationship show some of what she recalled in order to prepare to bitch at him. In the first paragraph she is working backward from age 3 to before her birth.

I am 3 years old. I visualize myself standing in the living room, watching my daddy read the paper. He has no time for me. I am 2 years old, sleeping on the couch while my father reads his paper. I am 1 year old, sitting in the grass with my mother while my daddy takes my picture. I am 2 months old. My daddy is taking my picture. I am about to be born. I am 8, 7, 6, 5, 4, 3 months old. How do I feel?

I am 3 months old following conception. I hear my father shouting. He is saying, "Goddamnit, Alice, I don't want any children. You talk to Mrs. Jones and find out who did her abortion. I want you to get an abortion." I am shocked. Why does my father want to kill me? What have I done to him that he hates me so much? My mother is crying. She defies him, and the rift in the family begins.

I am 6 months old. I just kicked my mother, and she is excited. She wants my daddy to put his hand on her stomach and feel me move. Daddy says, "That's silly. All babies move. So what?" I wish my daddy would put his hand on me. I would like him to touch me.

I am born, and my father is upset that I am a girl. He had his heart set on a boy. At least then he would have a pal, as he has never had any friends. He believes that my mother and I have played a nasty trick on him because I am female. If I had only been a boy, then maybe he could have loved me. I feel rejected. Being female is not OK. I begin to cry.

I am a year old. My mother leaves me with the neighbor couple while she goes shopping. The man plays with me. He puts a nickel on my toe, and it falls off. I laugh and laugh. I wish my daddy would play with me like that. Why doesn't he ever take care of me? I wish my daddy would take care of me.

I am 3 years old. My daddy gives me a nickel every Saturday for washing his back. He puts the nickel on top of the refrigerator so that I have to climb on a big chair to reach it. I wish my daddy would give me a big hug instead of money.

We are out for a Sunday drive. I am riding in the back, as usual. I want to sit in the front seat between my folks, like a love sandwich, Daddy-me-Mommy. My daddy always insists that I ride in back so I won't wiggle too much.

I am in the garage, watching my daddy work. He has such lovely tools. He has a cabinet full of hammers, screwdrivers, files, cans of nails, big boxes with interesting things like a lathe for mending shoes, and an emery wheel. My daddy is always busy and doesn't notice me. I begin to dump out the screws. He tells me I'm in the way, to run along and play. I would like to work with my daddy, to learn all about the different tools. But he is always too busy, too irritable. He makes me a lovely wooden teeter-totter. It is always leaning up against the wall in the garage. I want to play with it, but daddy says it is too much trouble to get out the saw horse, it might slip. Finally, I learn not to ask to play with the lovely teeter-totter.

I am 5 years old and starting to school. My daddy decides I should get a whole dime for my allowance instead of a nickel. But I must do something to earn it. He wants me to be his detective and tell on mother if she does something she doesn't want him to know about. One Saturday we are at the dinner table. My daddy wants to know whether I'm going to do my "detectin'." I whisper in his ear that mother and I went to the movies out of the grocery money this week. Both of my parents get angry, and I am in the middle. I feel that my daddy has tricked me into being a tattle tale. My mother spanks me for telling a secret. If my daddy were not so stingy, we would not have to slip around. If my mother were not afraid of him, we would not have to try to fool my daddy. We are all unhappy. My father has used me as a dupe. He does not respect me.

I am 6 and in the first grade. I am in a little play at school, but my daddy doesn't come. Later, I am in an evening program (or was supposed to be except that I have a big bandage on my eye where I got hit in the head with a baseball bat). My whole class is doing a Maypole dance, except me. My mother has made almost all the costumes. My mother and the neighbor girl and I go. My father is not there. I participate in many activities at school. My father is never at PTA, does not help with Bluebirds or Campfire Girls like my mother does. At church the Baptist preacher asks me to recite the Christmas story, which I know by heart. I do this in front of the whole congregation. My father is not there.

I am 9. We are getting ready to go to a movie. My mother and I are waiting in the car for my father to come out. He has to go to the garage, get out a clean handkerchief, go to the bathroom, get a cookie, etc., etc. At last he is in the car. We will be late for the beginning of the picture. My mother is mad. My father is eating an apple and ignoring her. They have already had a disagreement about what movie to see. My mother wants to see a comedy, and he has given in. The movie is very funny. My daddy slaps his knee, stomps his feet, and snorts. We come out of the movie. My mother says, "How did you like it?" He says flatly, "It was OK." I wonder why he won't say he liked it. What is wrong with having fun?

I am 12 years old. My father is teasing me again. He gouges too deep and hurts me. I scratch him with my fingernails and blurt out, "I hate you." He is thunderstruck; so am I. I know that I shouldn't say this, shouldn't criticize my parent, should honor my father. I stick this thought back down inside. I never bring it up again.

When my menstrual cycle begins, my father makes no comment. He never talks about sex except to make some remark, such as, "New York is sin city. All the people are immoral there. I can't understand why my sisters want to live there." He reads an article on sex and then says, "That's the filthiest thing I ever read." He is no help to me at all in discovering my womanhood. He is tight-lipped and rigid about sex. He equates pleasure with sin. I feel there is something shitty about me. My father is ashamed of my femaleness.

In my feedback to Laura I encouraged her to feel the depths of her yearning for her father, again to experience fully the little baby in her crying out, "Daddy, Daddy, where are you? I need you. Where are you?" Before summoning forth the buried rage, it is often necessary to recognize and give voice to the loneliness and deprivation suffered by the negative emotional child. I spoke to her first lovingly and gently, showing her sympathy and concern.

While she recognized her father's rejection of her, Laura's response to it was always muted by the Baygull programming she received from her mother. The next step for her, then, was to feel the depth of her pain and recognize how justified was the anger that went with it. With every line she wrote I stressed his cold and inhuman treatment of her, his stinginess, his heartless stomping on her expectations of love from him. As with the feedback to Chris and Nancy, my comments went beyond the general idea of his unlovingness to the specific instances she recalled in which his true nature was revealed. He put her on a seesaw of love by letting her wash his back and then making the nickel reward difficult to reach. He was inconsistent in his attitude toward her by building her a teeter-totter and then not allowing her to use it, all because of his compensatory guilt love. God forbid she should get hurt using it, then he would feel doubly guilty for causing her injury *and* not wanting her in the first place. I told her:

"Not only did he deprive you of his love, he ruined your relationship with your mother by coaxing you to spy on her. That bastard gave you no brothers and sisters, no real father, and then he topped it off by trying to destroy your relationship with your mother, all because of his little-boy jealousy.

"What's the matter with him? He couldn't let you sit between you and Mommy in the front seat? Did he hate you that much that he has to stick you in the back seat? You're a procrastinator. You're never on time. Where do you think you learned that negative trait? From that bastard who was always late to go anywhere. 'See, Daddy, if I'm late just like you, I won't outdo you. *Now* will you love me?' Don't you remember the times you went to the movies, and he found several opportunities to delay? You're just like him.

"How do you suppose you learned your perfectionism? You feel that nothing you ever do is right. He would permit you to mow the lawn, but you had to do it two or three times. It had to be perfect or Daddy wouldn't love you. Since then you have had to do everything over and over again to be perfect like your bastard Daddy demanded."

As the story of Laura's barren relationship with her father unfolded, her resentment of him became more open, although she was still not able to express it fully. Now, with the bitch session, the time had come for her to allow that rage and hatred to come forth. While most people find it easier to bitch at father than at mother, a few find that their fear of him is so inhibiting that nothing much comes out. In cases like Laura's it takes great effort by both the teacher and her to open up the wound and let the catharsis of the bitch session happen. During the group bitch session at the center she sat immobilized, insisting that she felt nothing. Rather than confront her resistance directly, I asked her to describe what she sensed was holding her back from bitching. Here's what she wrote:

> What is holding me back from bitching? Two things that I can think of straight off, which are really aspects of the

same thing. First, I am paralyzed with fear of men—my father to begin with, Jack my lover, and all men after that. This makes me afraid to bitch. It also makes me afraid of losing what I have—half a man, a crumb of a man, any shred of love I have or ever have had at all.

The second thing holding me back is the deep depression I've been in all week, which is precisely my sickness. This is my feeling, a deep conviction reinforced by years of negative thinking, that I never have been and never will be loved by a man. This overwhelming sense of emptiness, this pure need which has never been satisfied.

I have the feeling of being congenitally unlovable where men are concerned. All my life, since before my memory, I have felt inadequate, a zero, totally devoid of lovableness. I feel that it is totally impossible for me to have a loving relationship with a man I care about. Someone I don't care for might say he loved me, but it would be only words. In the area where it counts, down where I live, I am convinced, I *know,* that I can never be loved by a man I care about.

This black depression becomes a trap. Because of my intense, lifelong need for a man's love, I come on too strong, too needy, too helpless and hopeless. Men run in panic from this need which threatens to strangle or smother them. They can't or won't deal with it. Consequently, the greater the need, the greater the likelihood of my not getting it satisfied.

As Jack did not want to see me this week, his little "rejection" cast me into a funk—the "nobody loves me" syndrome. Of course he doesn't. Who wants a teary-eyed woman to make him feel guilty? Bitching at father makes it seem as if I am rejecting Jack, who is so much like father, and who is my last man, my last hope, half a man but better than none! The thought of losing the little I have makes me feel stifled, drained of energy, unable to bitch or get through the Process. I feel as if I'm being smothered, can't breathe.

After this special exercise and a further mind revelation, Laura saw that all her current problems were rooted in her father's failure to love her. With more work she was able to begin venting her pain and rage with real, animal-like ferociousness, beating on the pillows for several hours. Her anguished, wordless howls bore testimony to the pain she had suppressed for 35 years. Laura had many other bitch sessions that week, each directed at the specific scenes and traits she had previously recalled. Here is a small portion of one of those sessions:

> Daddy, you dutiful, cold bastard, I hate you for all the times you gave me your duty. *Your fucking duty. Shove your fucking duty.* How cold, narrow, sterile and unprofitable is your Goddamn duty. May you roast in hell for all the dutiful things you did for me—for your dutiful house, and dutiful meals, and dutiful clothes, etc., etc. *Crap on your dutiful shit!* If you'd ever given me *one ounce* of love or caring or support, if you'd ever given me a shred of warm, tender, caring recognition with all your duty, it might have passed as at least pseudo-love and I could have grown up secure. You sonofabitch. You stood in my way. You planted your feet and deliberately blocked my way. You with your sour face and sour looks and sour personality. The only word in your vocabulary was "no." You could never smile and say "yes." It can't be done says you. *Bullshit!* It *can* be done. It *will* be done. I shall live, am living, have lived in spite of you. If you don't like it you can shove it up your ass!
>
> The biggest thing I hate about you is the feeling you gave me of being abandoned, rejected, a zero, a nothing. I won't have it. I won't have it anymore! Instead of thinking of myself as nothing, as unworthy of love, of concern, of caring, I'll think of myself as a loving, caring, cared-for person that other people like. How do you like that? You don't like it, do you? You wanted me to go through life miserable, lonely, without a friend. Well, tough shit! It's too late because I've declared my autonomy from you. I won't be you anymore—self-rejecting, cold, unapproachable, snobbish, too good to speak to anyone. I won't be a masochist for you. I won't think of myself as miserable, a failure, a person that no one could ever love. Just because you didn't love me,

> you bastard, doesn't mean someone else won't. And I'm going to love him back, too—more than I ever loved you.
>
> I want to be free of you. I *am* free of you. Get your rigor mortis fingers off of me. I'm giving your corpse a proper burial. I am slamming down the lid of the coffin myself. "Let the dead bury the dead." Like Ruth coming out of the land of Moab, leaving the dead behind, I shall enter into a new land where love is waiting. So be it. Go to hell, Daddy!

To integrate further the effects of her bitching at father, I asked Laura to do a special mind revelation in which she asked her child to tell her intellect how she felt after bitching at father. This is what she wrote:

> I feel that father is no longer a threat to me. I see him there with his hands and feet tied to the stake (in her sanctuary), but he seems limp, unreal, like a ghost that turns out to be a sheet flapping in the wind, a corpse who is gone and has left behind only his shroud. There is nothing there. He is gone, who knows where? He was a towering monster, a King Kong, a hairy beast terrifying me with his roar. Then he became a tiny pip-squeak, a midget, a belch, a fart, a stink. Then he shrank away even farther to nothing. He doesn't terrify me anymore. I was paralyzed with fear, rabid with rage, indignant, victimized, frustrated. Now I can scarcely care. He is a rag flapping in the wind, a scarecrow. Who's afraid of a scarecrow? Who's afraid of the big, bad wolf? He's a fairy tale. A tale told by an idiot. Insane sanity. Illogical logic. I'm no longer afraid of his power. He's an imaginary bully. I said "Boo!" to him—and he vanished.

After upchucking father, Laura joined Chris and Nancy in a space similar to the one after having bitched at mother. They were totally relieved of the burden of their repressed anger from childhood—but they were not yet finished with father.

9. "Tell Me I May Sponge Away the Writing on This Stone!"

"I don't believe it is possible to defend that bastard," said one woman when she heard what was coming next. Father's Defense, like that of mother, requires an abrupt shift of view, which Baygulls and Zombies sometimes find too abrupt. They have been denied their chance to express fully their anger and resentment toward father for a long time. They feel so elated after being freed of the years of oppression and inhibition that they want to continue their rebelling and bitching.

Yet, to be effective the change must be abrupt. Turning the coin over to see its other side is a 180-degree shift. The bitching at father is one-sided, and a sudden shift to the other side drives home the impact of his defense in a way that a gradual shift of view would not. It is necessary to be catapulted into the bitching at father and then catapulted into defending him in order to shatter negative complacency. Bitching at father smashes all false beliefs in his positivity, while defending him transcends denunciation and replaces it with understanding.

Father, like mother, is guilty for not consistently loving you. But he, too, is blameless. To see this and stop blaming him is a crucial step in being free of his contribution to your negative love programming. One of the great ironies of the negative love syndrome is that children learn to blame and bear grudges from —who else?—mother and father. If those two never forgave an insult nor overlooked a misdeed, how could their children do otherwise than show the same lack of compassion and tolerance for others? If the parents never gave of themselves in a positive way, how could the children give positively to the parents in return? What tragic justice for everyone.

Those who carry grudges and nurse resentments often do so out of obedience to a parental admonition, either silent or overt, such as, "Don't let anyone get away with anything." Hostiles often have difficulty defending father for this reason. They sometimes need to be reminded that nursing self-righteous anger is always a negative trait of either mother or father. With this awareness the Hostile, too, can defend father.

Baygulls usually have a different problem. Mother and father have told them something like, "You should forgive people when they sin or do wrong because they cannot help themselves. They don't know any better. Be bigger than they are by forgiving them." Living by this directive serves the dual purpose of allowing the Baygull to feel superior while garnering the undeserved admiration of those who are fooled by his or her apparent piety. While appearing more pleasant than the Hostile, the Baygull's generous pose is just another false ego trip.

If you are a Zombie, however, you were probably programmed by your parents with such commands as, "Be quiet. Be safe. Don't show your feelings, no matter what." So the Zombie may have difficulty first bitching at father and then later defending him. Fortunately, once the feeling level is aroused, the energy behind it, like that of a flowing river current, can be channeled into a different course, and the Zombie can experience father's positive defense.

As with mother, a series of powerful mind revelations creates the Defense of Father. Seeing and hearing father as an adolescent boy describing his relationship with his mother and father is a totally absorbing, enlightening experience. The conversation with the 13-year-old child of father expands the view of him to encompass his total being. Children usually see their fathers only in the roles handed to them, rather than as complete people. Yet a person is not the roles he plays. By definition, the roles are what he is *not* and must learn to become. If father actually were a loving man, for example, he would not have to play a role. He would simply *be* a loving man.

While your father had many adult roles to play, (father,

husband, son, boss or employee, taxpayer, tourist, buyer, seller, teacher, student, or whatever), all that was only a small part of who he really was. For all his bluff and bluster, or meek silence, your father still had a hurt, frustrated child inside him, the same child in each of us who longs only to love and be loved. Underneath the big man who made your life hell was a frightened, angry, lost little boy who lived through hell himself and never recovered from it. The adult father you knew arose from the same kind of frightened, unloved, unfulfilled youngster you once were. Your father was a victim of negative love patterns as you were, perhaps even more so. He acted no more from his adult free will in treating you unlovingly than you act from your adult free will in not loving those around you. With your current adult awareness you can see beyond the role father played to the person he was underneath: an unloved, misunderstood child searching in the grown-up world for the love he never received as a boy.

Father did not love you consistently and positively because no one ever loved him consistently and positively. He therefore could not love you. It was beyond his limited ability as an emotional being to give you the warmth and emotional goodness you needed from a father. To continue to blame him is to show him an even greater injustice than he showed you. Love comes out of the fullness of one's being, never from the emptiness.

Father's Defense teaches you how to relate to father in spite of all the unloving things he did, not by saddling you with a Christian admonition you must struggle to obey ("Turn the other cheek") but by creating an emotional, intellectual, and spiritual experience of father's love tragedy so that you can feel compassion for him at all levels within yourself. Experiencing father's suffering, rather than merely intellectualizing it, causes anger to fall away.

Defending father must be a deeply emotional experience to make a permanent change in your attitude toward him. Reading about his negative love programming, as you are doing now, does not by itself give you the needed emotional experience, any more than reading about a cure for disease can make you well.

The Defense of Father is the same as the Defense of Mother in its three parts. First the negative emotional child psychically confronts the 13-year-old child of his father in the sanctuary. "Child of my father," he asks, "what was your childhood like? Where did you learn the negative traits I adopted from you?" The mind or psyche of his father then tells him the specifics of the pattern of lack of love in his life that created his programming to be the man he became. They converse in dialogue fashion, with father's child answering the specific questions put to him about each of the negative traits recalled in father's prosecution. For however long it takes to understand the origin of father's negative traits, the client continues to ask, "Where did you learn to be that way? Where did this trait come from?" As the answers unfold, it becomes clear that father was mistreated, abused and responding to the negative example set for him by *his* parents.

When all the information has been given in the Dialogue, father's psyche then dictates the story of his negative emotional autobiography in more orderly fashion. This Monologue is then followed by the Trial-log, the second "day in court" for the negative emotional child to bitch at father. In this procedure father, with his new understanding of his childhood programming, is able to defend himself. Should the client's negative emotional child get out of line, the spiritual self is present to act as judge-moderator to oversee the Trial-log. After these experiences one arrives at a place of understanding with no condemnation and compassion for father.

At this point in their Process work, Chris, Laura, and Nancy have finished bitching at father and are feeling the exaltation of their apparent victory over his lifelong influence on them. They have given the bastard hell for more than a week and have upchucked his negativity repeatedly until it is all lying piled in a corner of their sanctuaries.

The illumination of father's negative love background is similar to the light shed on mother a few weeks before. Since mother's defense was presented in great detail in Chapter 7, only a brief discussion of father's defense for each client is presented here.

In talking with his father's 13-year-old child self, Chris learned that his father's early programming at home had been even more Zombielike than his mother's. Chris's paternal grandfather had been a businessman, involved in running community affairs and aloof and withdrawn from his family. His creed had been work, duty, and propriety. At home he was emotionally absent, choosing to retreat from his son and daughters behind a wall of papers and books. While he was the image of manliness to the world, at home he was subservient to his wife, who ruled the house.

Chris's paternal grandmother, the source of the other half of his father's negative love programming, dominated his father's upbringing. "A self-righteous prig" was the way Chris's father described her in their dialogue. "She spent all her time on community things and charities, so I had to fend for myself. She didn't believe in 'coddling or caressing children,' so I learned early that crying would not get me any warmth from her." Later, his mother taught him to be condescending toward others and to behave in a coldly smooth, studied way that would bring credit upon her. She used to paralyze him with her critical stares. To gain what few crumbs of approval she offered, he learned to achieve and be a leader, do his duty, and ignore his own feelings and needs. Chris learned that his father was the son of an authoritarian woman who demanded that he deny his own feelings and live according to hers.

Learning at first hand the kind of parents his father had, Chris was able to make sense of the web of negative love from generation to generation. His father, like him, was programmed by both his mother and father to be a Zombie, feeling little and expressing even less. By understanding why his father programmed him as he did, Chris was able to substitute compassion for his dead father in place of the anger he felt during the bitch sessions.

By integrating what he heard in his father's defense with what he already knew about his mother, Chris was further able to see how both his parents had been programmed to be superior, unfeeling, undemonstrative, overly concerned with appearances, and unloving. While there were some differences in the programming of his mother and father, in many crucial ways each reinforced the "Zombieism" of the other for Chris. The negative traits first observed in Chris, his lack of trust, impatience, snobbishness, and overall critically disapproving, unemotional pose, were now traced back two generations on both sides of his family. In seeing the full negative love pattern spread out before him, and enduring the catharsis of first rage and then compassionate understanding for his mother and father, Chris dug out the roots of his negative programming and prepared to move to the next stage in learning to love.

Nancy also achieved a profound understanding of her negative patterns through her dialogue with young Charles, her father's child at puberty. To get a more complete picture of her father's negative programming, she listened as he dictated to her the story of his hard life as a poor farm boy in Kansas and, later, of the rigors and deprivations of life in the working-class slums of Pittsburgh:

"My father was a hard, tough man," he told Nancy, "a heavy drinker who disciplined us with his fists when we didn't jump to obey him. He was an angry man, and it seemed to me that he took little pleasure in his family or in anything in life except getting drunk, talking or playing cards with the other men, and women. Sometimes I felt that he didn't even know all our names for sure."

He explained to her that he had been the sixth of nine children, just one of the middle children in a large family that treated children as economic burdens and, later, as economic resources to be exploited, rather than as individuals.

Charles also told Nancy how his mother, her grandmother, had been a willful woman who silently resented his father for not giving her the luxuries she wanted. It was she who had engineered their move to Pittsburgh, and the children knew her as the real power in the house. Charles had briefly felt his mother's tenderness toward him during his infancy, only to be rudely supplanted by the next child as he was passed on to the uncertain care of the older children.

He also related to her the misery of their unstable, precarious life as a working-class family in Pittsburgh. Two of the younger children had died before age 5, and Charles felt his parents would not have cared if he had died, either. Loud, angry quarrels between his mother and father were an almost daily event in his home. His mother would castigate his father in front of the children, while manipulating the children into giving her the approval she failed to get from her husband.

Once she heard her father's story of deprivation and anguish, Nancy was able to see and feel the rest of the truth about her father. He was passing on to her the hurts that had been inflicted on him as a boy. From their Dialogue together, and then the Monologue and Trial-log, she was able to see the origin of the negative traits, moods, and admonitions he had passed onto her. His physical desertion of her mother, for example, had duplicated her grandfather's psychological desertion of her grandmother. Out of negative love to grandfather, her father had obeyed the silent but clear admonition, "Women and children are a burden to flee from." Similarly tracing through the heaviest patterns of negative traits showed her how the remainder of her father's unlovingness also resulted from the negative programming of *his* father and mother. Seeing her father as a young boy weeping inside with tears of frustration and loneliness served to call forth Nancy's own tears of compassion and sadness for the tragedy of her late father, who never knew loving fulfillment in this life.

When Laura reached her Trial-log, she, too, understood her father but had not completely lost her desire to condemn him for the hurts she suffered at his hand. In the Trial-log her child self had another chance to attack her father, who this time was permitted to defend himself against her charges. With the occasional help of her spiritual self as judge-moderator to keep order, Laura eventually relinquished her anger at father.

Among other things, she learned how and where her father had bitterly learned his rejection pattern. When her father, George, had been an infant, her grandfather had deserted the family and fled to another state. News arrived soon afterward that he had shot himself to death. While growing up, Laura had heard the story of her grandfather's suicide, but hearing her father's 13-year-old self tell it as he experienced it emotionally gave it a new dimension for her. What George explained, which she had not known before, was that he blamed himself for his father's death; that he believed during his childhood that his birth caused his father's desertion and self-destruction.

"I always felt that if I hadn't been born," he told her psychically, "he might have stayed with my mother and the other children. Maybe they would have had a better life if I hadn't come along to be another mouth to feed, another demand on him. If only I hadn't driven my father away!" Talking to the guilt-ridden child her father had been, Laura felt with him the hopelessness and self-hatred he had lived with all his life. While recognizing the error in his belief that he was responsible for his father's flight, she was also able to see that her father had lived his life as if it were true. For the first time she was able to enter into his experience and see the world as he did.

George described his mother as if she had been the old woman who lived in a shoe, with too many children and too much to do. He grew up feeling that life was a struggle and that laughter and pleasure were wrong and out of place in his home. He learned from his mother, Laura's grandmother, to lose himself in his work and avoid feelings, which were always painful in any event. George's mother programmed him to live by the old German ethic of hard work and little display of emotions.

From her grandfather Laura's father learned to abandon his family. George's father had physically abandoned his family, so George psychologically abandoned his daughter. Laura grew up feeling torn inside by her father's lack of love and acceptance, while resentfully believing that he could have given it to her if he had wanted to. After her father's defense, however, she understood that his programming from her grandparents left him totally incapable of loving himself, his wife, his daughter, or anyone else. He had received so many negative messages from his parents that he could only pass along rejection to his children. In attempting to rebel against her father's sourness and self-hatred, Laura adopted her mother's Baygull false buoyancy and cheer. Thus, Laura learned through the negative love pattern from her parents to restrain tightly her feelings of anger and hatred behind a mask of good cheer and ready smiles. She could not win.

As father's prosecution must be real to be effective, so his defense must be real to have a lasting positive effect. After the moving experience of his defense one is able to feel for the negatively programmed emotional child still trapped within father the adult. The experience of feeling for his tragedy must be so deep and intense that it makes a permanent imprint on the psyche, assuring that anger and resentment toward father are banished forever.

Father's compassion scene creates the compelling emotional experience necessary to replace anger with tender feelings for him. As with mother, the purpose of father's scene is not to feel grief over his death, which is a sad occurrence that no one can prevent. Rather, the compassion scene serves to evoke overwhelming grief and despair over the pathetic tragedy of father's entire life without love or fulfillment. When completely filled with tears and sorrow for father's suffering, one takes another step closer to loving him.

Like the others, Nancy experienced her father dying in the present, as a grown man with a small child trapped within him. She felt deep sadness and longing, not for herself at the death of her father, but for the poor man lying dead in his casket after living a wasted, useless, unloved and unloving lifetime. The compassion aroused in Nancy, as in all others who do this Process, was deep and genuine. Her father had actually died during her adolescence, yet she was able to experience him dying in the present and feel for him as if his death occurred today. These moments of sadness and pain, *for* father rather than *because* of him, helped re-educate Nancy's negative emotional child and her adult intellect. The funeral scene with father also helped motivate Nancy to rededicate herself to avoiding father's tragedy in her own life by finding peace and love in the work that still lay ahead of her. Here is a portion of Nancy's experience of her father's funeral scene:

> The attendants lower the coffin into the freshly dug grave and it comes to rest. I pick up a handful of dirt and let it fall through my fingers. As it hits the top of the coffin, I see the boy within the man, dead inside. My tears are streaming down my cheeks one after another faster than I can wipe them away.
>
> Poor hopeless little boy. You never stood a chance. Who mourns you? You had three children, yet except for me they neither know nor care that you are gone, and if they did, they would send a curse after you. Who has loved you, self-centered little boy having to pretend to be a man? You hated and mistreated, just as you were hated and mistreated by your parents. Now you are dead and this life's chance is gone. (Sobbing) You didn't want things to be this way! I wish I could help you! I want to help you. I want things to have been different for you. Oh, Daddy! Oh, Daddy! How I wish it could have all been different.

After experiencing the tragedy of father's life without love, there is another, more poignant, tragedy to consider: your own loveless life. Father's funeral scene is followed by your own. Project yourself 20 years into a future in which you have freely chosen not to rid yourself of the negative love patterns that have kept you from loving those around you, particularly your children. As the scene unfolds, you can see the bitter, angry children standing above your casket as it is lowered into the ground. Your living spirit is present as they curse you for passing on to them this dreadful negative love disease that has blighted their lives as it blighted yours. "Thank God, he's finally gone," they say. "We won't have to put up with *his* crap anymore. Jesus, I wonder how much money he left us in the will."

Does it make you angry or hurt to think your children will damn you when you are dead? Seeing and hearing, psychically, the faces and voices of those who have suffered because of your negative love to mother and father can serve to rededicate your total commitment to the task of learning to love yourself and others. As you cry over your own wasted life, there comes a moment when you stop and say, "Hey, wait a minute. *That's* not going to happen to *me.* I'm going to do something about this Goddamn negative love crap so that my children of the future will *not* stand over my grave saying, 'Go to hell.' They will cry over the loss of my loving companionship, but that's all. I *will be* loved and cared for, and *I will* be loving and caring."

At the end of *A Christmas Carol* Scrooge sees his own neglected grave in the future, with his name engraved on the headstone. With this glimpse of the "future," one can say, like Scrooge, "Oh, tell me I may sponge away the writing on this stone!" Dickens, too, understood both the deep anguish of seeing one's death in the future and the genuine rededication to a loving life that arises from this vision.

The mind revelation of your own funeral, like the others of the Process, translates your knowledge from the intellectual realm into core-level experience that you can feel and act upon. For Laura, Chris, and Nancy the worst is over. The Prosecution and Defense of Mother and Father is the toughest emotional ordeal anyone can face. It takes real courage to look at exactly who you are and purge yourself of the negative influence of your parents.

10. The Armistice

Did you make any resolutions last New Year's Eve? Did you tell yourself that this year would be different; that this would be the year you solve that annoying problem or drop that distasteful habit? What happened? Did you stick to your decision and improve your life? If so, congratulations! Deciding to break a destructive habit and succeeding are genuine achievements.

Most people did not do as well. They made resolutions and embarked on ambitious self-improvement programs of every kind, only to see their campaigns collapse in ruins within days or weeks. It started out well enough, with some early improvement and a bright outlook; yet sooner or later the old habit took hold amid self-condemnation, discouragement, and frustration. Whether that bad habit is overwork, overeating, smoking, drinking, procrastination, or the most common problem of all, the inability to love, most people are stuck in this familiar negative pattern.

Have you ever wondered why you go around this circle to nowhere? The answer is not to be found in lack of will power or discipline. The role of discipline and self-control in achieving our positive goals is vastly exaggerated.

For most of us, most of the time, the adult intellect and the negative emotional child are locked in bitter, self-defeating conflict. And the bad-feeling kid is winning!

Difficult as it may be to admit, the truth is that your intellect is not running your life. Despite your best intellectual efforts and all you have learned about "right living" or the "good life," (however you may define them), your life is being controlled by that rebellious, unloved child you were before you reached puberty. The more you struggle to control the child with discipline, the more frustrated you become, because of the negative love syndrome.

The emotional child controls the adult intellect. You did not leave that kid behind when you grew up. Most of us are not the civilized adults we pretend to be, endowed with the ability to make rational choices. Instead, we are mostly overgrown emotional children, *pretending* to be thinking adults. Behind the intellectual façade rages the fury of the emotions we felt as children. The intellect is like a mere speck on the ocean of emotion, for it cannot control the child within. Each time the adult intellect attempts to make a change that the emotional child opposes, the little bastard inside throws up obstacles, resistances, psychosomatic illnesses, excuses, lapses in memory, anything it can to defeat the best intentions for change.

The consequences of this battle within the self are widespread and devastating. Psychiatrists' offices, therapy groups, meditation classes, the entire spiritual growth and human potential movement, are filled largely with people searching for an end to the pain of the conflict between what they know and what they feel. The inner turmoil, confusion, pain, and distress caused by this conflict rob our lives of its joyful promise. We neither think to our full potential nor feel all that we might because when the intellect and child do battle, both are losers.

Although the worst of the emotion-intellect conflict occurs in adulthood, it begins before puberty, since the prepubertal child has a modicum of intellectual understanding along with the programming he receives daily from mother and father. He has some knowledge of right and wrong, and he knows what creates harmony and disharmony at home. Even as he is employing the crooked maneuvers his parents are teaching him through negative love patterns, the individual knows there is something better than the way he is living. As he grows up, he learns more and more with his intellect about the loving potential in human relationships, even if he never saw it at home. "Other families were not the way mine was," he may discover with pained surprise. "There really *is* something better than the life I knew as a child." When he tries to outdo mother and father, though, he experiences with full force the impact of the split between his intellect and his emotions. What he thinks he wants eludes him, while what he gets is what he thinks he does not want. In truth, while his adult intellect watches helplessly, he gets exactly what his negative emotional child wants.

Unfortunately, the adult intellect remains the struggling victim of the emotional child even when it understands the damage brought by the conflict. When the individual becomes a physiological adult, the intellect continues to grow and mature, while the emotions remain stuck in childhood. As the years pass, the gulf between them widens and deepens, creating an almost constant state of tension, anxiety, and confusion. After puberty, within severe limitations, the intellect can use its free will to act negatively or positively, depending on its responsibility, desire, and training. Usually it unknowingly and ignorantly chooses to live out the negative programming under the control of the childhood emotions, saying something like, "That's the way I am. I can't help myself." Such a statement is one of the lies we adopt because of our negative love patterns. We are *not* the conflicts and negativities we adopted from our parents. But the power of the negative emotional child is such that it does not permit the intellect to cut the puppet strings of negative love to mother and father.

It is important to dispel the myth that you can "Be a parent to your child," as if there must be a child within you for the rest of your life. The child is only a metaphor for the negatively arrested part of your emotions. The goal of the Fischer-Hoffman Process is for the child to grow up and no longer need parenting. You *can* get a loving divorce from mother and father, but in order to do so you must recognize that the emotional child within does not have to, and definitely should not, remain inside, messing up your life. Nor is it true that you are stuck with the cards your parents dealt you in your childhood. You can always choose to do something about it. Better to spend your energy helping that childish part of yourself grow up than to carry it around like a pet affliction.

Getting clear of mother and father, therefore, is not enough to end the debilitating conflict between the intellect and emotions. Mild feelings of depression and incompleteness tend to persist at this stage of the Process. The adult intellect, therefore, must defy the emotional child and force it to stop causing trouble with its negative antics. Knowledge is power. The intellect gains this power to defy the child with its newly acquired understanding of its problems.

Until the adult intellect learns that the real source of its problems is the negative emotional child, it is powerless to change. It can struggle valiantly and achieve small, hard-won advances, but it can never gain lasting victory until it identifies and engages the real enemy. When the intellect does understand the true cause of its problems—negative love patterns—it can procede to take responsibility for redirecting its life by opposing the force of the programmed child. "I am going to fight this resistant little child that is wasting my life," it decides.

This decision, when joined with determination and commitment, is not simply a New Year's resolution, soon to be broken. It inevitably creates more tension, however, for it presages a new confrontation: the adult intellect versus the emotional child. The anticipation of any battle is a period of tense preparation. The emotional child is insecure and fears giving up its games. The habit forces that drive it are powerful, and it resists the unknown future. For its part the intellect is righteously indignant at the emotional child for all the grief and misery it has caused. This combination of fear and anger is part of the natural uneasiness one feels even after being clear of mother and father. There must be nothing tentative or hesitant in this new battle. The intellect must stick to its decision to prevent the child from continuing to behave in its negative patterns. Only in this way can the internal conflict end once and for all.

The next step, then, in learning to love oneself is for the adult intellect to take on its negative emotional child in a bitch session. Here the intellect attacks the child's destructive, resistant behavior and demands that the child stop playing the negative tapes from childhood that are delaying their mutual progress toward fulfillment. Most of all the child must stop blocking the way of the adult intellect's efforts to make a better life for itself through wisdom and learning. The re-educated intellect knows what is best and what it needs and is angry with the negative child for preventing attainment of these positive goals.

The adult intellect begins to assume control over the negative emotional child through a mind revelation in the sanctuary. The intellect takes the child firmly and decisively in hand and says, "Look here, youngster! It's *you* who are to blame in this, not mother and father. *You're* doing this to me, and I want you to cut it out. Your nonsense has ruined my life long enough. Your negative garbage has caused all my problems. You've carried a grudge against everyone and fought with me, and you won't let go. You're *still* fighting with me. I don't need that negative love crap in my life any longer. From now on you're going to do what *I* say so that we can learn to be loving and happy."

To illustrate the dramatic resolution of the child-intellect conflict, I have drawn from the Process work of Chris, who we have already seen in Chapters 5 through 8.

Chris, like many clever, well-informed people, experienced tremendous discomfort because of the contending parts of himself. He was quite sophisticated in various therapies and growth systems, yet they had been largely intellectual experiences for him. Beneath his intellectual understanding of his own and other's problems, he had a severely arrested emotional child who effectively manipulated him away from any lasting solutions to his love and work problems.

After a mind revelation to prepare him, Chris's adult intellectual self was able to bitch with great feeling at his negative emotional child. (By this time he was no longer a Zombie on the Rocky Arc of Emotion.) Here are portions of the notes he made about that session.

CHRIS: INTELLECT-CHILD BITCH SESSION

You're a child, but you're a bad one. You are misbehaving, and I am going to tell you what you've been fucking off about. I am supposed to be your intellect, and I'm a hell of a lot smarter than you are, and I know where it's at, and I'm telling you to shape up. You have been fucking us over, been mechanical, playing your Goddamn roles. Whenever it gets a little tough for you, you stupid twerp, you clam up. You cannot say what's on your mind. You won't express your feelings openly. Then what do you do? You can't even make a Goddamn decision. You fuck us over. Suspicious and distrustful, that's what you are. If somebody doesn't quite accept you totally, you see it as total rejection. But no more. I've had enough of you. Too damn much!

Doubter! You refuse to believe in anything or anybody. Every time you face somebody who has a little authority or power, you back off, clam up. You can't make a decision. You paralyze us.

It's our life, you dumb little weepy twerp. Well, you're not going to be afraid of your shadow anymore. No more doubting, no more indecision. You're going to listen and understand how we've been hurting because of you.

You think you've got self-love? Bullshit! What you have is fear. You're a frustrated chickenshit. And when you can't have your own way, and you get a little scared, what do you do? You give me hay fever, headaches, colds, you dumb, self-defeating little brat! And you think your fine appearance and a Goddamn cardboard fake image is what's going to protect us, but it doesn't. It just fucks us up and gets us hurt. I'm going to pound some sense into your head, you spoiled, negative brat.

Now you're going to listen to me. No more crap. Stop your games. You stamp on others and then turn around and play "overresponsible." You think you have to take on the whole Goddamn world. Let's have a little response to *me*. We're going to confront each other and grow up. No more running away. Grow up, you dumb, self-defeating, suffering bastard! You do not avoid conflict by running away.

I'm going to make you listen to me. No more sabotaging my growth, you little bastard, do you hear? Love to argue, do you? Think you're right and other people are wrong? Well, I know where that comes from, and you know where that comes from, and you're not going to keep it. I won't buy it anymore. *You can't dominate me anymore.*

(Crying) You bastard, you dumb, negative, self-defeating shit! Resent me if you like, but you're not stopping me and you're not turning me off. No! No! I won't let you. I will not tolerate your sabotaging me anymore . . . You're always right, and you're always afraid, and you start and never finish and your wishy-washy vacillating never lets you make a decision yourself.

Child, you're bad! You really are powerfully bad . . . and I don't want to go through life like this, not loving, always dominating and selfish. You're the spoiled-rotten, negative image of all the rotten negative traits of your father and your mother.

Afterward I had to throw up, and while throwing up, I focused on my child's negativity, not him. I feel so clean, not empty but clean inside and light. I feel so much cleaner than I did before—more, even, than after dealing with Mom and Dad. I don't feel anger, which was a defeated or frustrated quality to me. I'm feeling he won't really try so much anymore, and if the little bastard does, I'll take care of him.

Chris thus cleared himself with his child. In this session he unloaded the residual anger he had been carrying around since his defense of father. Once the child had been bitched at completely, Chris prematurely felt that he had gained stewardship of his life. He felt as if he had finally whipped the ogres that had plagued him for so long. The delicious feeling of conquest was short-lived, though. He was stunned out of his self-satisfaction when told that the least suspected character in this life mystery is actually the most guilty.

The true villain is the intellect, who has just basked in the glow of victory over the child. It is far more guilty than the child because it shifted responsibility and blame everywhere except where it belonged, on itself. It blamed mother, father, the child, society, anyone it could in order to avoid seeing its own negligence and culpability. The intellect failed to take responsibility for its life and allowed the negative emotional child to act up and create the problems it then struggled in vain to solve. The intellect also made no effort to experience or understand the child and what it needed: understanding with no condemnation and compassion. Instead, the intellect made life hell for the child without mercy or restraint.

As we did with mother and father, we must abruptly look at the other side of the child-intellect coin. In a mind revelation the intellect is tied to a tree in the sanctuary, giving the child freedom to defend itself fearlessly against the earlier charges of the intellect. The child berates the bound and gagged intellect:

"Yes, I'm guilty for programming you, big smartie intellect.

Yah, I adopted all those negative traits from mother and father, *but you permitted it.* I was unaware and didn't know any better. You learned right from wrong. *You* were supposed to know better. You were smarter and bigger, and with your awareness your job was to help me and control me. No wonder I don't wanna grow up. I'm staying split from you because you're no friend to me. You never really cared for me. You never loved me. You just used me as a scapegoat to avoid taking responsibility for yourself. The hell with you! If you won't care for me, *who will?*"

The crucial discovery in this procedure is that unless each part of the self accepts and understands the other parts, the total self is divided and schizoid. The child, rejected by mother and father, has also been rejected by the intellect. All his life he has felt like an unwelcome guest in his own house. Now comes his opportunity to air his lifelong resentment at the treatment he has received at the hands of his intellectual self.

Thus primed, Chris's child was ready to defend itself and put the responsibility and blame where they now rightfully belonged. Here is an excerpt of how Chris's child turned the coin and bitched at his tied-up intellect.

CHRIS: CHILD INTELLECT-BITCH SESSION

> OK, Mr. Big Man Intellect. You're tied up now, you S.O.B. You bawled me out; now it's my turn. You told me it was all my fault that we were getting screwed up and that I did this to you. Sure I did it to you. I fucked you over good to get back at you. But you're supposed to be the big man. Christ, I'm just a little kid. I counted on you to tell me what to do and make sure I did it, so I wouldn't get into trouble and feel so Goddamned guilty. And you, you just left me alone. Well, it's your fault, too.
>
> Jesus Christ! I haven't the words to argue with you. If I had the words to argue with you I'd *be* you; you're my other half. I need you, you bastard, and you sit back and judge me and tell me to be something I'm not. Well, I am what I am. If you want me to shape up, then you help me by understanding me, not by being critical.
>
> You talk about how I hurt you. You have only a little feeling. I hurt 20,000 times more than you. *I need your*

help. I need you and you need me, damn it! I'm smart enough to know that. Without me you're a big hunk of dumb cement. Without you I'm just a big hunk of feeling, and I don't know what to do or where to go. When you shit on me, I'm going to shit back on you twenty times as much. I can't help it, and you can, you bastard. You must help both of us. Let me know it's all right and that you'll take care of us. . . . (Crying) . . . *I can't do it alone! Damn you!*

Following these two bitch sessions, the intellect at the child and the child at the intellect, it is possible to resolve the problem of who is responsible for the unloveability. Both recognize that each was guilty but blameless, for neither one knew any better due to the negative love programming. Having heard the enormous pain behind the plaints and grievances of the child, the intellect becomes humbled and contrite. It realizes the truth of what the child has been saying. With guidance it recognizes the need for a truce. The gag and bonds are removed, and the intellect is free to respond. It walks up to the child, puts an arm gently around it, and says something like this:

"Hey, little one, I never saw it from your point of view before. You're right. I know you weren't guilty. And I know I wasn't guilty, either. I'm sorry for rejecting you. Let's stop fighting and get together. What do you say?"

The emotional child by now also recognizes that it has been at war with its intellect all its life. It, too, is tired of fighting and wants peace. Yet at first it approaches the idea warily, since it has suffered greatly from the condemnation and lack of understanding from everyone, especially the adult intellect. The child tends to reply cautiously, saying, "I'll try if you will." Here is how Chris experienced the truce between his emotional and intellectual selves:

CHRIS: CHILD-INTELLECT TRUCE

CHILD: You hear me, Mr. Big Shot? Do I get through to you? Hey, man, I can't go on like this without killing us both. And I don't want to do that. (Crying) You gotta help me, Big Shot. I'm taking the gag out of your mouth. Talk to me.

INTELLECT: Look, child, I hear you. Finally I hear you. You're right, I was stupid and a thickheaded jerk. Little Chris, I cannot go back and change the past. Now I understand. I've let you bluff me. I haven't taken care of you. I haven't taken care of us. Now that is changed, and it's going to be different. I understand you now clearly, and I don't condemn you. Sit here next to me. Let me put my arm around you. (Both are now crying.) We may have our differences, but I'll help you shape up. I'll lovingly explain where it's at. I've always copped out on that and just cursed at you. And, as deep as I can feel, I'm sorry. I won't do that anymore. I won't let you scare me. I won't back off. If you need to be confronted, I'm going to confront you. When I'm hurting you, confront me. No more fighting, please. How about a truce until we learn to love?

CHILD: Yes. (Crying) Yes. It's been so long. That's all I wanted. Yes, I want a truce. I'm tired of fighting. And you better damn well mean that you care, that you won't run away again. You're going to have to prove it!

After the truce the emotional child begins to accept both the friendly motives of the intellect and the possibility of leaving behind its immaturity when it grows up. With its modicum of intellectual ability the child recognizes there is no longer any cause for it to remain childish. It has prosecuted and defended mother and father, it has ended its conflict with the intellect and now has no legitimate cause for its dis-ease. The child fully understands that it no longer has to live according to the old adopted negative love games. Having experienced this crisis, it is free to choose the positive alternative.

The intellect has also reached a crisis point. At long last it takes responsibility for its past failure to exert control over the child and give it support.

Thus, the intellect and emotions finally learn that each is not the natural enemy of the other. The war is over.

11. The Joy of Play

The state of truce is not yet love. Although the hostilities have ended, and the groundwork for further growth and friendship between the adult intellect and the emotional child has been laid, more is needed. To consolidate the hopeful but cautious peace, the two lifelong adversaries need to learn to play together.

What does *play* mean to you? What part of your life do you consider to be play? Is your play truly lighthearted, joyous, and carefree? Can you play, both alone and with other people, in a way that renews, relaxes, and makes you feel good about being alive?

Most people cannot play in this positive way. Instead, they do playlike things for serious, unplayful reasons. For example, if you play golf to beat your opponents, or to make business contacts, or perhaps to escape your unloving family, you are engaging in negative play. Unlike positive play, it doesn't leave you more inwardly renewed and play-full, for negative play only creates more anxiety and tension.

Those who say, "It's no fun unless I win," miss the point completely. Competition destroys the spirit of play. When it is really play, the score does not matter. Much of socializing at bars and getting high with a few ounces of alcohol is also not play, since its goal is the assuaging of loneliness and the hope of finding a bed partner. The need to buy attention or approval in play, as in work, stems from the negative love syndrome. Those who feel unloved and unlovable carry that burden around with them wherever they go.

Some people consider their work play. That is a misunderstanding. Work is like play in that it can be either positive or negative, but it is always done for a goal. Positive play is its own goal. Building a swimming pool is work. Splashing in the water is play. Both are needed for a balanced life.

In positive play the spontaneous, childlike aspect of self is set free to enjoy its inner flow of activity. Whether tearing around a tennis court or quietly listening to some favorite music, true play is done with a deep sense of ease and fulfillment.

Sadly, many children never played with pleasure. Either they were alone, feeling unloved and rejected, or they experienced play only negatively by fighting, throwing things, and disrupting the good times of others, all as part of the negative love conditioning from their unloving parents.

As an adult, playing is as important as anything you can do with and for yourself. If you never experienced positive play as a child, you will find it impossible to enjoy the richness of adult life. Without play you will not only miss much of the fun in life, but you will also not experience your own happy self as a natural part of you. But, you may say, childlike playfulness is only a role we sometimes adopt to fit in with others; the "serious" me is the real me. The truth is exactly the opposite. The real you is joyous, while the somberness is something you adopted and learned to live with, to gain your parents' pseudo-love. If you rarely laugh with genuine delight, never tell a joke, and in general feel little joy in life, it is certain you have never learned to accept some of the finest human qualities as your own.

The saving grace is that despite your negative play experiences in childhood and the unplayful habits you may have developed in adulthood, you can learn to play happily and freely. You can be reunited with that childlike part of yourself you may have forgotten. Or never known. Just as the emotional child can learn to stop its negative behavior, so the adult intellect can learn to accept and enjoy the child's positive, childlike amusement. To be whole again, the adult must simultaneously become less childish and more childlike. To be of benefit, play must be a direct experience. Only by seeing and feeling the long-obscured happy self does the adult intellect accept and acknowledge this most valuable part of itself: the carefree, lovable child.

All this is experienced on the evening of the play session, which is a happy highlight of the Process. The preceding 11 weeks have consisted of hard work and truly soul-searching experiences designed to purge negativity. On this evening the classroom is transformed into a festive play room, gaily decorated as if for a birthday party. Elaborate preparations assure an evening of special memories. The entire three-hour session is a party, with each client as a special guest.

The party begins with a mind revelation in which the group leader has the adult intellect take the emotional child on its lap and ask the child to teach it to play. The child agrees and is elated with its new, positive responsibility to teach its adult intellect the joys of play. The session then becomes a combined birthday and Christmas party, with all that the heart of a child longs for: games and toys and good things to eat, lovingly prepared and shared. They romp and laugh together, tell stories, and dance. The entire group enters joyfully into the spirit of the evening.

As the play session draws to a close, the adult intellect again takes its emotional child on its lap and thanks it for teaching it how to play. It tells the child how great it will be for both of them when it grows up and brings its happy, childlike positivity into the adult Trinity. The adult intellect knows now that joy and seriousness, laughter and responsibility, fun and commitment, can all be part of life in the present. For its part, the emotional child now truly realizes that it is not going to be harmed or further criticized and condemned. It understands that it is only being asked to drop its childishness, while retaining its positive, childlike qualities. The emotional child loses nothing except its pain.

If misery loves company, then joy loves company even more. The play session gives clients an opportunity to share positive experiences with others in a social setting. After playing together, they learn the truth, that others want to reach out to them and share joy with them if they will allow it to happen. To enjoy oneself alone is not enough, for if it is to be full, life must be shared. The play session is the turning point of the journey toward reintegration of the Quadrinity. Through direct experience both the emotional child and the adult intellect learn that the negativity of a lifetime was completely adopted from outside and that the true self is both positive and joyful. Once this truth is fully comprehended, change for the better is inevitable.

In contrast to earlier sections of this book, the play session notes in this chapter are filled with the lightheartedness of a happy child. Nancy had played as a child and was sometimes able to play as an adult. Secretly, however, she condemned herself for it. She considered play to be childish and irresponsible because her negative emotional child still lived within her. As a result of her play session experiences, however, she learned the life-enhancing value of positive play:

> It was like a beautiful fantasy, but it was far more than that. It was a reality that I helped create, because it was me as I am now and me as I am becoming. I felt close to all the people there and connected to the children in them and the child in me who now sees life with wonder and fearlessness. This was the child I knew was there. This was the exuberant, wonder-full child that had been denied. I'm so glad she's still around. My wish is to have this part of me stay in close touch with my adult intellect, each trusting, each willing to share the strengths they have with each other.

At this point the relationship with mother and father can be re-evaluated from a new perspective. Were they really all that bad? Did they not do anything loving or tender in those first 13 years? Of course they did things right, many times, even if only through pseudo-love. In preparation for learning to love mother and father, it is necessary to uncover and relive those moments from the past when they were affectionate, protective, and caring. Even the most negatively programmed person can find some positive scenes from childhood. Writing the Positive Emotional Autobiography with Mother and Father serves to balance out the negativity of the prosecution and defense. Unlike the earlier negative emotional autobiographies, no goading with rude questions is necessary. When one is relieved of negative love and defensive forgetfulness, he has no difficulty recalling beautiful moments from the past. Now, after prosecuting and defending her parents and learning compassion for them, and for herself, Nancy is ready to see them in a different light. Here she recalls some of the happier times from her years before puberty:

NANCY: POSITIVE EMOTIONAL AUTOBIOGRAPHY

My mother is sewing a dress. The material is fine and white, and she is taking such care to make all the stitches tiny and even. My father is sitting just out of the ring of light at the table. He wonders at Mother's pleasure at having another baby when the other two have been so painful and worrisome. He feels proud of her and hopes everything will go well with this baby. This baby is me, and the dress is for me.

(At age 2) We all take a ride to see Grandma's family. Mother and Grandma take turns holding me in the car. It is breezy, and I squeal. Daddy likes taking everybody in the car and Mother wants her aunts to see *me.* That's nice. I know she thinks they will like me. I love bouncing around in the car and feeling the trees zoom by. When we go by a post, it sounds as though we cut it off, just with the sound . . . Zap. It's nice to go bouncing along all together.

After washing up for supper, my father puts Hinds Honey and Almond Creme on his hands. There is too much, so he takes my hands between his and gives me some of the warm, smooth stuff to use on my hands. Then we go together to the table, both smelling the same, both ready to eat supper.

In the kitchen, wrapped in a big towel after my bath, I feel warm and safe. My mother has my nightgown hanging over the heater in the other room, and when I get dry, I will have a warm, dry nightie to put on. My father made popcorn for us. My brother is practicing the piano, and it makes happy tinkling sounds.

My sixth birthday. My mother makes me a pretty dress, red with white polka dots, and she laughs when I ask her how she made it without my finding out. She shows me where she has kept it while she was working on it. My father takes us all to the zoo in our new car. We stop for gas in the city, and when my father says it is my birthday, the man gives us each a sucker. I am pleased and proud.

On Halloween, when I am 6, my mother and father get

us ready to go out. Mother helps with the costumes, while father shows me how to make a noisemaker out of a spool with notched edges and string to pull it, so that it can be put up to a window. When the string is pulled, the spool edges make a loud noise. Then he burns a cork and blackens our faces with it. We are given a flashlight to carry.

Later on, mother keeps us feeling like a family. We go on lots of Sunday picnics, some of them at a beach. I can still smell the special wet smell that goes along with swimming as a child: Mother and the other grown-ups sitting in the shade, my brother bringing buckets of water from the lake so I can make sand castles. I remember the lovely, gritty egg salad sandwiches and the ride home in the open car, everything filled with sand, my toes scratching in my sandals, everyone relaxed, sometimes singing things like, "Row, row, row your boat!"

There is something special about thunderstorms in the summer. We all sit together after running around to close the windows. My mother counts the seconds between the flash of lightning and the sound of thunder, and we try to figure out how far away it had been. I love it, feeling excited and safe.

My mother loves to listen to me telling her about the books I read. She seems really interested in them, not like she is judging whether or not they were "good" or "instructive" but in what seems to me to be a rather childlike manner. This is a new idea to me. It is a sharing with her that I am unaware of at the time. Her interest is not as an adult thinking, "What a bright daughter," but as another human being on pretty much the same level.

She was the one who encouraged and supported me because she was *there* with me. I realize that a lot of positive relationships were there with my mother that I have not been aware of. I have ignored my mother's warm human role in this, not being perfect, just interested. They were both really doing their best.

The importance of these recollections is the opportunity they afford to reconsider the past unclouded by negative love patterns. For the first time in adulthood Nancy saw her childhood years with genuine appreciation for the goodness those years held. She can describe her early years without intellectualizing or covering over any unacceptable feelings of anger, fear, or resentment. She knows exactly what happened and how she feels about it. She is free of negative feelings about her childhood and will carry the good feelings with her for the remainder of her life.

After writing her positive emotional autobiography, Nancy found herself feeling more positive than ever before. Her depressed moods began to lift, her body posture straightened, and her facial expressions took on a new brightness.

To further solidify the newly positive attitude toward mother and father, clients are asked to describe how their parents' virtues have affected their lives positively. Here is how one young man described his insights.

> My parents were both active, athletic people, and from them I learned to enjoy my body and keep myself in good physical condition. My father was strong, quick, and well-coordinated, and he taught me to love physical exercise. I love playing tennis and baseball, as well as any good physical workout, thanks to the example he set.
>
> Both Mom and Dad loved beauty of all kinds. They appreciated subtlety and detail, qualities I have adopted in my photography. My father was original and inventive in solving problems. Many times in my life I have felt great satisfaction in solving problems or creating new designs that have flair, simplicity, and beauty, the qualities he loved most.
>
> Best of all, my parents loved to laugh and smile. Like them, I love telling good stories and laugh easily. People like my hearty laugh and ready smile. The laugh is my father's, the smile is my mother's. God bless them both for the beauty they passed along to me.

The play session and the positive emotional autobiography provide a solid foundation for the integration of the Quadrinity in the Closure session.

12. Closure: The Day of Re-Birth

The negative love syndrome survives on the vain hope that someday our parents will finally love us. All neurotics hope that somehow they will finally gain a resounding "Yes!" to their unspoken childhood plea, "I'm just like you, Mommy and Daddy. *Now* will you love me?"

These hopes are sad and pitiful. Negative behavior does not lead to positive love. No matter how much like them you become, or how tirelessly you struggle to rebel and rise above their negative example, mother and father will never love you the way your emotional child needs and wants: selflessly, wholeheartedly, and with nothing asked in return. One empty cup cannot fill another. Until you see this truth, you live helplessly imprisoned in darkness. You can search for love endlessly outside yourself, but as long as you continue to look for mother's and father's love from the past, you are stuck there and cannot go forward.

You have been on a long journey of discovery. You have learned that mother and father are the source of your love problems, yet are blameless victims themselves. You know you have been at war with yourself. You have learned that to be fully alive is to be able to play. All of this has been preparation for the ultimate truth: God's love is inside you, waiting to be set free, once you remove the learned negative patterns that block its expression.

When the lie of negative love has been exposed, it must fall away and die for lack of nourishment. Once the inner void is filled with genuine self-love, the motive force behind the negative patterns disappears. Why vainly seek pseudo-love from the past when you can give true love to yourself in the present?

Of course, there is nothing new in saying that the answer lies within. Psychiatry, the human potential movement, and various religious disciplines all give voice to this wisdom. How frustrating it is, then, to search in vain within yourself for life's most highly prized experience. If love is inside us, why can't we find it?

Not until the puppet strings from mother and father are cut, and love is uncovered on the emotional, intellectual, and spiritual levels, can you find your own source of love.

Dr. Julius Brandstatter, an old friend and Process teacher, has aptly expressed this idea.

"Negative love is passed from generation to generation in almost all people and families. Is it any wonder that we have a sick and getting-sicker society? The corrections begin with oneself. And the most evil of all evils is negative love. It is a sickness in itself, alarmingly contagious, reaching epidemic proportions with no immunity for anyone. Until this is understood, there is little chance to arrest this virulent disease which threatens to engulf everyone in time."

In replacing negative love with true love, there is the culminating event which we call Closure. After dropping the negative love traits, the positive emotional child still remains separated from the rest of himself. The child within must now be helped to grow up and take his place as a loving, integrated aspect of its adult mind Trinity. Everything that went before has been preparation for this climactic step.

This major life event is marked by a ceremony befitting its significance. It is a celebration of love and renewal. The colorful clothing of the graduates blends with the lovely floral setting. Everyone is joyful with the great sense of achievement.

The Closure mind revelation lasts two and a half hours, yet seems like minutes. It is a solemn affirmation of loving commitment to oneself. One stage of life is ending; another is beginning. The ritual serves to seal the agreement with oneself to leave the negative realm of the past life and willingly emerge into the new life of positive self-acceptance and love.

Learning to love is accomplished by teaching the adult

intellect and the emotional child three final steps. They are (1) acceptance, (2) forgiveness (in which "Turn the other cheek" is no longer an admonition from outside but an internal state of being experienced on all three levels of mind), and (3) uncompromising love. The child finally receives the love it needs from the most important being in its existence, *not* mother or father, but its *own* adult self. Here lies the essence of the self-love experience. With no negative blocks to prevent it, love flows freely between the two selves, adult intellect and emotional child.

In the final session, the actual love exchange begins with a mind revelation taking the child back year by year to infancy. The emotional child relives the highlights of each year until it reaches age 6 months, where it finds itself sitting in front of its intellectual self, crying out with agony at re-experiencing those loveless years. The suffering of its emotional child evokes total empathy and compassion within the adult intellect. It reaches out for its child, lifts it into its arms, feels the warmth of the baby's body, and tastes the salt of its tears. Knowing the child is neither guilty nor to blame (for it did not know what it had done), the adult intellect expresses its heartfelt understanding with no condemnation. It experiences compassion, acceptance, honest forgiveness, and true love. The infant's cup of love is filled from the most important being in its world, its own adult intellectual self. The emotional child's quest for self-love is finally realized.

The child is now willing to grow up. The intellect and spiritual self watch as the child gradually grows, year by year, receiving their positive love. Tears of joy and relief flow freely as the child feels, for the first time, the warmth of complete acceptance. Beginning with this moment, the child within *feels* love as a total experience.

Finally, the emotional self arrives at the same chronological age as the adult intellect. There is now a positive emotional adult in place of the negative emotional child. As they lovingly face each other in their sanctuary, they again share the five steps of love: understanding with no condemnation, compassion, acceptance, forgiveness, and love. They then lovingly embrace, fuse together, and become wedded as one. This new duality then merges with its spiritual self and becomes a totally integrated mind Trinity. Experiencing the spirit merging with the intellect and emotions fills one with a sense of transcendence and union with the infinite. The summit has been reached.

The mind Trinity has been relieved of negativity. With this new, solid, centered state of well-being, the Trinity is ready to make lasting peace with mother and father and share love with them. (The experience is valid whether mother and father are living or dead.) The re-educated and loving Trinity completely understands that mother and father were not the cause of negative love patterns, merely the innocent transmitters. Therefore, the mind Trinity stops blaming the parents, who were unwitting carriers of the dis-ease.

First mother's spirit is brought into the sanctuary. The new Trinity walks up to her, embraces her, looks lovingly at her, and says, "Mother, dear, I understand now who you are better than you have in all your lifetime. I don't condemn you anymore. Mother, I have found real compassion for you. I accept you and forgive you, for you did not know what you did to me, to father, or to anyone else. With all my heart, I give you my love."

Then father's spirit is brought into the sanctuary, and the love exchange is repeated. They embrace, and the Trinity says, "Dear father, I know and understand you now with acceptance, compassion, and forgiveness. And I love you."

Giving love to mother and father is the final step in cutting the puppet strings and achieving emotional autonomy and the loving divorce. If the parents are dead, their nonphysical mind spirits and yours can experience the beauty of this sharing. If they are still alive, the loving exchange is repeated face-to-face as soon as possible following Closure.

With the final mind revelation, the newly integrated Trinity rejoins its physical body to become a Quadrinity. Closure is complete. The newly cleansed mind Trinity can now reprogram the computerlike brain to behave positively.

The Process is an emotional catharsis, involving radical cleansing and purifying. It has been likened to emotional surgery with no anesthetic. The final mind revelations during Closure "suture up" wounds opened during the prior month's experiences. As with any injury or other shock to the system, one needs time, rest, and quiet to recover totally.

The death of negative love patterns does not bring an immediate end to negative behavior. Habits of a lifetime, both positive and negative, die a hard death. The persistence of negative patterns after their cause has been removed is similar to the phantom limb phenomenon, in which an amputee continues to feel as if the severed arm or leg were still there. The gradual pace at which some negative patterns disappear is similar to this neurological phenomenon.

Consider the common example of a man who moves from one home to another. One evening shortly after the change in residence he leaves a party and heads for home. He absent-mindedly drives toward his old home instead of his new one. The habit pattern from former times took him the wrong way. The same sometimes holds true for the negative love patterns.

To continue with this example: When the man realizes what he is doing, he says to himself something like, "Oh, what am I doing? I don't belong on this road anymore. My new home is elsewhere." He then turns the car around and heads in the right direction. One does the same with negative behavior patterns when they recur after the negative love syndrome is gone. One sees these patterns as unrooted, psychological lies from the past, puts awareness on them for what they are, and deliberately alters his direction to suit his new circumstances. With each recognition of the pattern it becomes easier to be free of it. As one becomes aware of old negative traits, he can say, "Oh, yes, that's another old game I adopted from mother and father. It's groundless. Who needs it?" Then he can let it go.

To help eradicate the psychological lies from the past, various mind revelations are used to recycle negativities to positiveness. Some of these techniques are described in Chapter 4.

For those who experience them, the return of the old ways can seem frighteningly and discouragingly real. Awareness and patience are needed. Like erasing a chalk mark on a blackboard, the first cleansing stroke will make the image fainter but not completely obliterate it. Usually the second or third swipe is sufficient to clean it completely.

Without roots the negative trait cannot survive the regular use of recycling techniques.

For recycling and awareness to be effective, however, one must choose to use them. One can either use the techniques to consolidate his gains or remain the victim of the now-false negative habits. One man experienced his responsibility for his future in this way:

During the week I heard my perfectionistic doubter say, out of negative love to both my parents, "Bob's mind revelations are simply auto-suggestion, they don't have any substance. I can make them fail if I want to. They are not perfect techniques." Later I understood how right I was. If I want them to fail, I lose. If I want them to work, I win. They can work if I want them to, for otherwise I could not have done the bitch sessions and every other aspect of the work, which had such a profound effect on me. So I want this final mind revelation to work so I can get it all together. Then I recalled the orange and lemon mind revelation and how I salivated, and I realized that this was not just fantasy. Why did I salivate when I ate the imaginary lemon? Could I make the mind revelation and still fail final processing? Yes, I could, but I won't. I'm going to win. For my problems have been with my mind, so I will accept the mind revelations to cleanse my mind.

Win he did. This man is an internationally acclaimed concert musician. Prior to the Process, he experienced tremendous anxiety before going on stage, even though his performances were flawless. His hands perspired, and his mouth went dry from his extreme nervousness. Today his stage fright is gone, and he performs with self-assurance and relaxation. A recent newspaper review praised not only his musical genius but also his poise and stage presence.

When the new state of love is consolidated life changes are dramatic. Problems of unlovability, fear, guilt, anxiety, despair, anger, and psychosomatic illnesses begin to vanish. Not surprisingly, experiencing true love also changes one's attitudes toward relationships of all kinds. Husbands and wives either draw closer together in love, or they separate lovingly. Those who love truly also relate more lovingly and positively with their children. Having discovered how negative love patterns crippled them in childhood, parents are especially determined not to pass them on to their children. They also report with obvious delight the willingness of their children to respond to their new, loving parenthood.

One such response came from the grown daughter of a 56-year-old woman who went through the Process: "Dear Bob,

My mom has become a real mother to me, filling my life with much love and joy and comfort. She credits this development to you and therefore I thank you for all you've done for us. Sincerely, Betty Silverman daughter of Janet Silverman." She appended the following postscript: "When the tree bears fruit, the gardener smiles and rejoices in the success of his efforts . . ."

Perhaps most dramatic of all is the new-found ability to love one's own parents openly, even after many years of separation, confrontation, or pseudo-love. You can no longer be negatively affected by them, because you no longer have "buttons" for them to push. At the deepest levels of our being we want to exchange love with our parents. Removing negative love patterns clears the way for this to happen.

With love one also learns to accept people. When they are negative one is able to understand the truth behind their façade and therefore be more understanding while avoiding entanglement in their patterns of negativity.

How is it possible to be so positive in a world so negative? Even if you love yourself, how can you live lovingly in an unloving world?

Refusing to live fully in the world until it is perfect is another aspect of the negative love program from your parents. When the mind Trinity is re-educated and rid of the blinders put on it by the childhood emotions, one sees that the world is not perfect, but simply the way it is. Each of us has power over only a small fragment of it. The great spiritual teachers of the past, Moses, Buddha, Jesus, and Mohammed, could not eradicate the unloving evil in the world. It is enough to eradicate the evil in oneself.

Moreover, the world may not be as unloving as you think. Patterns of negative love close our eyes to much of the goodness and warmth around us. All you see is what you know. If you knew only fear, anger, jealousy, and stupidity as a child, that may be all you have allowed yourself to see as an adult. Once you experience love on all four levels of being, you are able to see the love in the world around you.

Achieving self-love and love for others is both powerful and beautiful, but it is not a "high." Peaks of elation are often followed by valleys of despair. True love replaces this cycle of highs and lows with a broad plateau; and from this plateau you can climb to still higher plateaus.

This does not mean that you will never have moments of unhappiness, grief, righteous indignation, or pain. Living well means flowing over the obstacles and experiencing them without being overwhelmed.

The death of a close relative or friend, for example, may leave one grieving for the loss of companionship. With self-love, however, death no longer brings severe depression and remorse for past wrongs left uncorrected or deeds of kindness left undone. In the workaday world, too, when things go against you, either through miscalculation or the dishonesty of others, your response of acceptance and determination to know better the next time will stand you in good stead. Righteous indignation at those who treat you unfairly is valid. Being rejected by someone to whom you want to give love may also bring temporary sadness, but with true love for yourself it will not lead to depression.

Those who experience the journey through the patterns of negative love to the transformation of self-love write of the aftermath with simple power. The following report, highly abbreviated, relates the experience of one of the "reborn."

> Immediately following Closure I felt drained. I told myself, "This isn't as much different as I had expected." I did feel something else going on inside of me, some further, undefined, internal process that had been started but certainly not finished.
>
> Later I got depressed and angry, with a feeling that this whole damn painful Process had been just one more search for magic like a Goddamn little kid, and here I am let down again. This feeling came and went for a week or more. I even felt resentful at having a last assignment to write up the final session.
>
> Gradually I became aware that I was changing. I continued to follow the post-Process homework prescriptions. Throughout the Process I had been more and more aware of playing invalidation games with myself and other putdowns. Now, after the Process, these habits are losing their control over me. I tried to revert to my old ways of feeling and seek escape by telling myself that I was not really responsible for my life and that the world was too big and

complex a machine for powerless me, but these didn't work. I was stuck with the knowledge that I was really in charge of my own life.

Looking back now, some time after Closure, I can see changes in me, many that I feel inside and some that other people have told me they see. I spent much of my life being sick and exhausted in bed. I have not been sick since Closure. No colds or flu. Some seasonal hay fever has persisted, which I am confident will also go as I learn better how to care for myself.

I feel more confident in all areas of my life than ever before. The myriad little questions and paranoid fears that add up to "Suppose he or she gets mad at me" or "Am I OK?" just don't occur much, and when they do, they are obviously so silly that they fall apart when I look at them and use my post-Process tools.

All my life I have hidden and felt personally attacked and threatened whenever someone disagreed with me. Now I find myself listening, and agreeing or disagreeing openly, without my habitual defensiveness or attack.

The frustrations and barriers which I met in the past still occur, but my depression over them does not. Most of my life people have told me, or shown me, that I appear cold, uncaring, aloof, and critical, at least until they got to know me. And with a front like that, not many people made the attempt. In the past months, people have commented on my approachability and caring and made comments like, "You've gotten so loose. It's great!"

Prior to the Process I avoided being with my mother out of anger and fear. I paid holiday "duty calls" and always with a heavy feeling of guilt, intolerance, and a desire to get out fast. She pushed my buttons so strongly I often couldn't get in her door without feeling zapped, and phone calls left me seething and swearing and taking it out on my family.

Ever since the Process I have felt comfortable with her and have expressed my love for her. I have actively taken care of her and felt warm and loving. She still says the same things and complains in the same way, with her subtle and not-so-subtle put-downs. I see them clearer than ever, but now the old instant rage/guilt/attack/run away feelings don't follow. She's just a human being with wants, needs, pains, feelings, and habits like anyone else.

Although my father died early in my life, I have at last made my peace with him. I am sorry he died before I could physically experience his warmth and have a chance to be a living, loving friend with him.

I am becoming a firmer and more supportive father to my three daughters. My wife has told me of the great changes she sees in me. She says I am much stronger, a trait she describes as a mixed blessing. She can count on me more, but it is harder to manipulate me. She also describes me as being much more sensitive to her moods and feelings. My old ways of denying myself, hiding, and not telling her how I felt about things are changing now, too. Our relationship, which was wooden, dependent, and unreal, is turning into a vital human exchange between two live people.

I now know and feel to my depths that no one is responsible for my life except me. What I do is up to me. The real barriers and limitations I meet are not out there but within. Like it or not, I am in charge of my attitudes and my life —and I like it. I have long periods of respect and love for myself I rarely experienced before. I wish everyone could experience the best of what I have experienced the past two years.

Lastly, I want to say that nothing is finished. I continue to change and grow. My life is flowing, and I am on a journey, not knowing quite where my path goes but joyously content to follow my heart.

Here is how Tom, a young law student, described a visit to his parents shortly after Closure:

As soon as I arrived home, I saw that on my parents' side nothing had changed. I saw all the old patterns, but instead of participating in the insanity, I felt understanding, no condemnation, compassion, total acceptance, forgiveness, and selfless love. I felt better every day I was home.

The first day I was home, Mom was rushing around trying to get things ready for Christmas. I told her I had something important to tell her, and she had to be still. She said, "Son, even the important things in life have to be sandwiched between. . . ."

"Well," I said, "I just want you to take a couple minutes,

put things aside and listen. I want you to *hear* me." Finally she stopped. The difficulty in getting her to stop for a minute only increased the feeling of compassion I had for her. We were sitting upstairs, and she had her arms folded across her belly. She was very tense and started crying a little.

"I want you to relax and hear me, Mom."

"I can't relax! I listen the way I want to!"

"Okay, that's fine, Mom. I understand. Mom, I just wanted you to know that I love you."

"Is that all?" she asked incredulously.

I took her in my arms. "Yes, Mom. You know that I will *always* love you."

"You don't have to say that. Always. That's implied." I understood her anxiety about "always."

"I do love you," I said. As I held her and gave her my selfless love, she let go a big flood of guilt.

"It was stupid to have you as a child when I was so young." She was crying as I held her, feeling the flow of love between us. I knew I *could* give love and giving it felt wonderful.

"I am 48, and I'm still not grown up," she sobbed. "But you're 26, and you seem to be all there."

"Right on, Mom. I am all here, and I love you."

"You feel like you're all together, like somewhere along the line you picked up the ball, like you picked up the load."

"Right on, Mom!"

"You had me worried that you had some disease or something was terribly wrong. I'm glad you told me that you love me. I love you, too."

That night Dad was in bed reading the newspaper before he went to sleep. I was trying to think of how to make "I love you" explode into his heart and mind. I was wrapping some gifts, and I thought, "The time is perfect. I don't want to wait one more minute. I want to give this to him now." So I went into his room, and this is what happened:

"Dad, there's something important I want to tell you." He put down his newspaper. "Dad, I just want you to know that I love you," and I took him in my arms and kissed him. It felt very warm, with no big explosion. I felt understanding, no condemnation, compassion, total forgiveness, acceptance, and selfless love for Dad during the whole visit. The "I love you" was just part of that continuum. Before I left, Mom said she couldn't understand it. I hadn't been so loving since before my brother was born when I was four.

Some months later I made my decision that I wasn't going to follow Dad's footsteps and become a lawyer, but intended to build houses instead. Mom and Dad became anxious and uptight. Instead of lashing out defensively or closing up, I just continued to give them both my selfless love. That love eased their disappointment and helped them to accept what I was doing. Our relationship has been beautiful ever since.

After having reached this state of love for self, their parents and others, people are able to make the positive long-term changes in their lives they have only dreamed about before. Like Tom, they may move into more satisfying lines of work, or else they may find new ways of relating to what they are already doing. Their present love relationships either become closer (as Chris's did) or they are able to separate from the man or woman who is not nourishing to them and create a new and fulfilling relationship.

This letter arrived at the Center just the other day:

Dear Bob,

It has been just a year since I finished the Process, and I am fulfilling your parting request to let you know what happened to me.

The news is unbelievably good. I have finally achieved the kind of loving relationship with a woman I always longed for. I'm no longer fearful and rejecting of women as I used to be. The Hell of self-doubt and emptiness is gone. My tendencies to be suspicious and judgmental as an excuse to reject people have evaporated. I'm no longer on guard all the time. I can remember laughing, joking, and exuding enthusiasm as a cover-up for my old negative feelings when I was with people—and then going home and feeling so lonely and inadequate that I'd have fantasies of killing myself to end the pain. All that is done and gone. Thank God for Fischer-Hoffman!

Bob, everything has changed for me. Now when I have a good time with people, either at work or socially, it's for real. I keep feeling good after I've left them. I've grown sure of myself and open to other people. For the first time in my life I have both men and women as friends, and life seems very good. Loving Sally happened in such an easy, flowing way it seemed the most natural thing in the world. We are friends, companions, lovers, and roommates, and we plan to get married soon. We are happy together and we want to give to each other because giving feels so good. Just like you said, it's as simple as that.

She loves the country as much as I do. Just last month on our trip to Oregon we found the piece of land we've both been dreaming about, and it is going into escrow next week. We expect to be ready to move there for good in a couple of years.

We both send our love and deepest gratitude and our hope that you will come to our wedding. All my love,

Carl

Words pale next to experience. Reading brings knowledge, but experience brings *knowing.* When you experience the truth of self-love, you will find that *you* are the answer you have been waiting for. You no longer need to search for love or struggle to gain it from others. When you learn how to find the source within yourself, you can drink from your own cup of love and share the joyous overflow.

Afterword

This book is meant to be an introduction to the Fischer-Hoffman Process. It is not an end in itself. It was written to show how negative love patterns are the root of all emotional problems and how one can gain lasting freedom from them through this brief, intense experience.

We at the Center hope that specialists in psychology, psychiatry, criminal justice, and education will evaluate this material and investigate its worth. We hope that it will soon find its place in the experiential training of all those in the helping professions.

Those responsible for our courts and prisons know only too well the devastation of the negative love syndrome, although not until now by that name. The failure of rehabilitation and the high rate of repeat offenders derive directly from the failure to overthrow the emotional cause of all criminal behavior: the negative love syndrome. With self-love and self-respect, criminals, like all other neurotics, can leave the negative past behind them and become loving human beings.

The negative love pattern could be aborted early in life if the Fischer-Hoffman Process were taught in our schools. Ridding 14-year-olds of their negative attachment to their parents would enable them to face positively the task of preparing for a life of love, work, and play. I hope that parents, teachers, and school board members will see the need for the most important subject in any educational curriculum: *love.*

There is an age-old pattern in which a few men and women have originated an idea; passed it along to others with high hopes for the betterment of mankind; and then watched with dismay as the original has been watered down and corrupted. We hope this unfortunate pattern will not be repeated with the Fischer-Hoffman Process.

There are many splinter groups claiming to be qualified to do our work. The Process is like powerful medicine; it can be dangerous in the hands of those who are not specifically trained in its use. Only those who have been thoroughly trained at our Center are qualified to teach it.

For more information about the Process and teacher training, write or call:

Hoffman Quadrinity Center
1005 Sansome Street
San Francisco CA 94111
(415) 397–0466

Appendix: "The Doors Will Open"

I did not learn about negative love—and its fundamental importance as *the* destructive force in our emotional lives—by studying psychology or by practicing psychiatry. I have no background in these or any other behavioral sciences.

The story of how I learned about negative love and how to eradicate it still fills me with wonder. Even today, it seems incredible that I, of all people, should be chosen to receive and disseminate the life-enhancing knowledge and techniques described in this book. Certainly, "chosen" is the correct word, for I did not seek it out. It came looking for me.

My life had been quite ordinary and unfulfilled. I was a businessman in Oakland, California. Like many people who were young during the Great Depression, I wanted the financial security I had missed as a child. I had a wife and small son to support, and all my time and energy went into business. The post-war years were economically good ones in the Bay Area, and I became successful.

Like most people, I also had many of the negative love patterns described in Chapter 2, with no understanding of where they came from or what to do about them. In short, I was a typical person of my age and background: part of the 98 percent who don't know how to love.

In 1961 the late Rose Strongin, a lovely sensitive and spiritualist teacher, helped me discover and develop my natural psychic abilities, which served to transform my life. What began as merely a fascinating hobby played an ever-increasing role in my life as I experienced frequent, dramatic episodes of clairvoyance and clairaudience. In the beginning I did not always understand how I did it, but I was clearly able to tune into the living minds of people whose bodies had ceased to exist.

The world of psychic phenomena was still only an interesting diversion from my business life until a fateful night in January, 1967. I awoke around midnight with an uneasy feeling. At first I thought someone was in the room with me. Then I realized I was receiving a spirit communication. As I focused my awareness, I clairvoyantly "saw" Dr. Siegfried Fischer, a friend who had died six months earlier. In life, Dr. Fischer had been an orthodox psychoanalyst, neurologist, and scientist who did not accept the concepts of parapsychology and psychic phenomena. Many times over dinner in my home we had argued about the existence of a living mind after death. During one such debate I had said, "Siegfried, you're in your seventies, you know. Chances are you'll go before I do. One day you'll see that I'm right." Then I added laughingly, "When you wake up and find yourself dead, come back and say hello."

When Dr. Fischer appeared that night in 1967 I wasn't really surprised to see him. I had been communicating with the minds of the so-called dead for several years. I was happy to see my old friend, I acknowledged his presence, and we briefly discussed the fact that he was still living in the mind realm. I thanked him for coming and was ready to go back to sleep.

"Wait, Bob," he said. "There's something I want to communicate to you." I sensed a note of urgency.

He then told me, in essence, that he had learned why he and his contemporaries in psychiatry had not had the total success they would have liked in finding a resolution to emotional problems. He also said that he now had access to a great fount of wisdom, and that he had developed a technique that offered the resolution so many people sought.

"That's great," I said, somewhat bewildered. "But wouldn't you be better off telling this to a psychiatrist? I can't be of any help to you."

"Oh, but you can, Bob," he replied. "I need a psychic channel to work with, someone with whom I have a rapport. You and I are friends, we can communicate and together establish this knowledge."

"Siegfried, I'm flabbergasted," I said. "Almost everyone I know already thinks I'm a little strange because of my psychic development work. How will anyone listen to me as an authority on emotional problems? I really know nothing about these things."

He countered with, "Yes, that's true now, but you'll find opportunities where you can help people. Just trust me."

"Well, I need emotional healing myself. You know all the problems *I* have."

That was no understatement. I was well aware of what a poor husband and father I was. I didn't really like myself, let alone love myself. I felt insecure, uncertain, and often depressed. There had never been any genuine love in my life, and if Dr. Fischer had something that would solve my 44 years worth of problems, I was willing to see what it was. Since he wasn't going to charge me $50 per hour, I flippantly thought to myself, I had nothing to lose but a few minutes sleep. Little did I know what awaited me.

"OK, Siegfried," I said. "Whatever this new technique is, start with me." For the next five hours Dr. Fischer took me on an excursion through the rudiments of what became known as psychic therapy. Dr. Fischer removed the "blinders" that had kept me from seeing the source of my emotional problems: my negative love attachment to my mother and father. I saw, psychically, all the scenes of my childhood that programmed me to be neurotic, unloving, and unlovable.

Next, he astounded me with what has become one of his greatest contributions to modern behavioral science. Dr. Fischer showed me how to relive psychically the childhood of my parents to see how they, too, were programmed to be neurotic and unloving. I saw my mother's childhood in Russia. I saw her poverty and unhappiness during her formative years. I saw how her life, like mine, had been nothing but hard work and no love; how her parents, like mine, did not know how to give her the love she craved. It was to get away from this emptiness that she married very young and came to America. Then I saw my father's childhood, also in Russia. He, too, came from a large, poor family, and I experienced his emotional poverty.

When I saw my parents' childhood scenes and their abject need for love and security, my anger turned to compassion and understanding for them. As much as I had suffered, they had suffered far worse from their parents. I saw all of this clairvoyantly while hearing Dr. Fischer clairaudiently explain it to me. At the end of the five-hour session, he psychically reunited me with my parents, and I was finally able to exchange love with them. I cried for all the years I had wasted trying to get love from them and everyone else in my life. I was overwhelmed with joy that at last I had made peace with my parents. I no longer had to prove anything or continue to bear a grudge against them.

When we finished that night, I understood that Dr. Fischer *had* found the answer to emotional problems. What he had discovered was not just the cause of our difficulties, but the cause of the cause, our parents' childhood experiences. They, too, were the victims of unloving parents, as I was.

At the end of that fateful session, I was reborn. But it was still unclear to me how I could do for others what Dr. Fischer had done for me. In the days that followed, we communicated further as he continued to clarify and refine the basic techniques. I repeatedly asked him, "But Siegfried. What am I going to *do* with this? Who is going to listen to *me?*"

Always the answer would come back, "Bob, who used to worry, mother or father? Don't worry. The doors will open."

Soon I began teaching the Process to the psychic development groups I had been conducting as a hobby. I discovered with great surprise that everyone had virtually the same basic emotional problem: the inability to love himself and others.

In 1969, my early work began to receive serious attention from the medical and psychiatric communities. During a talk to a group of doctors, psychiatrists, and psychologists, I met a psychiatrist named Ernest Pecci. He was a student of metaphysics and was especially interested in how I psychically read the childhood of parents who had been dead for many years. A few weeks after that first meeting, Dr. Pecci phoned to ask if he could refer one of his patients.

"I have a woman I would like you to see. She hallucinates, seeing ugly faces and hearing horrible voices. She hasn't been able to sleep without taking pills."

As a psychic, I was familiar with the problem of negative psychic forces intruding in the mind's realm. I willingly agreed to see her. During my session with her I used a technique Dr. Fischer had taught me for removing the negative mind forces that had been invading her brain and causing her to experience the hallucinations. (The technique is a variant of the guide and sanctuary process described in Chapter 4.) After one session she was free of her distress and had the tools to guarantee it did not return. She also resumed sleeping without medicine.

Soon Dr. Pecci and other physicians began sending me more of their problem patients. I was able to help them with Dr. Fischer's techniques. I began meeting regularly with Dr. Pecci and discussed with him the details of what Dr. Fischer had taught me. Dr. Pecci validated the effectiveness of my work from a psychiatric point of view. Word spread that the psychic process was enabling people to make radical, positive changes in themselves. The work load quickly grew far beyond my ability to handle it. I sold my businesses and established consulting offices. The waiting list grew and I began searching for a way to use the psychic process more efficiently.

One of those who knew of my work and wanted to experience it was Claudio Naranjo, a Chilean psychiatrist who had come to Berkeley and established a higher consciousness group called Seekers After Truth (SAT). Claudio experienced the Process, accepted it, and dubbed it the Fischer-Hoffman Process. He began to offer the Process in encounter style with one of his SAT groups. When I observed this group over several weeks, I was impressed with Claudio's courage and willingness to experiment, but I knew the encounter style was wrong for this work. The solution to people's emotional problems is within themselves, not in other people. Claudio agreed with me.

In late 1972, Dr. Fischer showed me how the Process could be improved and made more efficient by combining group lectures and one-to-one consultation. In January, 1973, I used this new format with a group drawn primarily from my waiting list. Once each week I lectured to them on the concepts and premises of the Process. Originally, I had read psychically for my individual clients while they listened and took notes on what I told them about their childhood experiences and those of their parents. In the new Process, each person learned to read psychically for himself. This gave greater credibility to what they learned.

Most recently, the Process has evolved to include the more active participation of the spiritual self, the part of the Trinity that originates in the Godhead and already knows how to love. This added dimension helps clients to recognize and use their own strength and wisdom from the very beginning.

Since the Process moves by stages through a clearly defined structure, it was necessary to be certain each person had successfully completed one stage before moving to the next. Written assignments and individual consultations as needed assured everyone's timely progression. This concept, too, proved exceedingly successful in practice.

Most recently, the Process has evolved to include the more active participation of the spiritual self, the part of the Trinity that originates in the Godhead and already knows how to love. This added dimension helps clients to recognize and use their own strength and wisdom from the very beginning.

There is an ever-growing demand for the Process. I now spend my time conducting the Process and supervising teachers, as well as training professionals for future groups. To this day, Dr. Fischer, through me, continues to improve and refine the Process.

People in behavioral sciences have told me that our Process contains a synthesis of many of the ideas of the world's religions, philosophies, and higher consciousness movements, as well as variations of theories and techniques used by Freud, Jung, Perls and Berne. Wherever it came from, I'm grateful that it works. With the advent of the Fischer-Hoffman Process, you need no longer embark on a life-long quest for emotional peace and love. As this book shows, once the negative love patterns are removed, you are completely free to love yourself and others, thus ending the search.

Yes, Dr. Fischer was right. The doors did open.

Since I received the Process I have become a minister, and as such am privileged to teach others how to find God's love both within and beyond through this method. Our teachers at the Quadrinity Center are either licensed psychotherapists or ministers.